**New Directions for
Community Colleges**

Arthur M. Cohen
EDITOR-IN-CHIEF

Caroline Q
Nathan R
ASSOCIATE EDITORS

Amy Fara Edwards
MANAGING EDITOR

D1524280

Constructions of Gender

Pamela L. Eddy

EDITOR

Number 179 • Fall 2017
Jossey-Bass
San Francisco

Constructions of Gender
Pamela L. Eddy (ed.)
New Directions for Community Colleges, no. 179

Editor-in-Chief: *Arthur M. Cohen*
Associate Editors: *Caroline Q. Durdella, Nathan R. Durdella*
Managing Editor: *Amy Fara Edwards*

New Directions for Community Colleges, (ISSN 0194-3081; Online ISSN: 1536-0733), is published quarterly by Wiley Subscription Service Inc., a Wiley Company, 111 River St., Hoboken, NJ 07030-5774 USA.

Postmaster: Send all address changes to *New Directions for Community Colleges*, John Wiley & Sons Inc., C/O The Sheridan Press, PO Box 465 Hanover, PA 17331 USA.

Information for subscribers

New Directions for Community Colleges is published in 4 issues per year. Institutional subscription prices for 2017 are:

Print & Online: US$454 (US), US$507 (Canada & Mexico), US$554 (Rest of World), €363 (Europe), £285 (UK). Prices are exclusive of tax. Asia-Pacific GST, Canadian GST/HST and European VAT will be applied at the appropriate rates. For more information on current tax rates, please go to www.wileyonlinelibrary.com/tax-vat. The price includes online access to the current and all online back files to January 1st 2013, where available. For other pricing options, including access information and terms and conditions, please visit www.wileyonlinelibrary.com/access.

Delivery Terms and Legal Title

Where the subscription price includes print issues and delivery is to the recipient's address, delivery terms are **Delivered at Place (DAP)**; the recipient is responsible for paying any import duty or taxes. Title to all issues transfers FOB our shipping point, freight prepaid. We will endeavour to fulfil claims for missing or damaged copies within six months of publication, within our reasonable discretion and subject to availability.

Back issues: Single issues from current and recent volumes are available at the current single issue price from cs-journals@wiley.com.

Disclaimer

The Publisher and Editors cannot be held responsible for errors or any consequences arising from the use of information contained in this journal; the views and opinions expressed do not necessarily reflect those of the Publisher and Editors, neither does the publication of advertisements constitute any endorsement by the Publisher and Editors of the products advertised.

Publisher: New Directions for Community Colleges is published by Wiley Periodicals, Inc., 350 Main St., Malden, MA 02148–5020.

Journal Customer Services: For ordering information, claims and any enquiry concerning your journal subscription please go to www.wileycustomerhelp.com/ask or contact your nearest office.
Americas: Email: cs-journals@wiley.com; Tel: +1 781 388 8598 or +1 800 835 6770 (toll free in the USA & Canada).
Europe, Middle East and Africa: Email: cs-journals@wiley.com; Tel: +44 (0) 1865 778315.
Asia Pacific: Email: cs-journals@wiley.com; Tel: +65 6511 8000.
Japan: For Japanese speaking support, Email: cs-japan@wiley.com.
Visit our Online Customer Help available in 7 languages at www.wileycustomerhelp.com/ask

Production Editor: Shreya Srivastava (email: shsrivsata@wiley.com).

Wiley's Corporate Citizenship initiative seeks to address the environmental, social, economic, and ethical challenges faced in our business and which are important to our diverse stakeholder groups. Since launching the initiative, we have focused on sharing our content with those in need, enhancing community philanthropy, reducing our carbon impact, creating global guidelines and best practices for paper use, establishing a vendor code of ethics, and engaging our colleagues and other stakeholders in our efforts. Follow our progress at www.wiley.com/go/citizenship

View this journal online at wileyonlinelibrary.com/journal/cc

Wiley is a founding member of the UN-backed HINARI, AGORA, and OARE initiatives. They are now collectively known as Research4Life, making online scientific content available free or at nominal cost to researchers in developing countries. Please visit Wiley's Content Access Corporate Citizenship site: http://www.wiley.com/WileyCDA/Section/id-390082.html

Printed in the USA by The Sheridan Group.

Address for Editorial Correspondence should be sent to the Editor-in-Chief, Arthur M. Cohen, at 1749 Mandeville Lane, Los Angeles, CA 90049. All manuscripts receive anonymous reviews by external referees.

Abstracting and Indexing Services

The Journal is indexed by Academic Search Alumni Edition (EBSCO Publishing); Education Index/Abstracts (EBSCO Publishing); ERA: Educational Research Abstracts Online (T&F); ERIC: Educational Resources Information Center (CSC); MLA International Bibliography (MLA).

Cover design: Wiley
Cover Images: © Lava 4 images | Shutterstock

For submission instructions, subscription and all other information visit:
wileyonlinelibrary.com/journal/*cc*

CONTENTS

EDITOR'S NOTES

The first volume of *New Directions for Community Colleges* (NDCC) on the topic of gender in community colleges was edited by Barbara Townsend in 1995. This seminal work focused on the role of power in 2-year organizations and how this power was influenced by and in turn influenced social identities of gender. At the time, this work was groundbreaking as it provided a snapshot of the experiences of women in community colleges—a perspective that heretofore was absent in the literature. Consider at the time that only 13% of women were college presidents (American Council on Education [ACE], 1986) and that gender was still viewed predominantly as a binary—men or women—versus the more complex understandings of gender present today.

Women have comprised the majority of all college students since 1979 and have held half of community college faculty positions since 2003 (National Council on Education Statistics [NCES], 2013). Yet, women remain less represented in leadership ranks as currently only one of three community college presidents is a woman (ACE, 2012). In 2008, Jaime Lester edited a second NDCC volume focused on gender in community colleges. This volume sought to extend the work that Townsend and colleagues presented as well as broaden the discussion of gender to include issues facing men and masculinity. It is fitting that this new volume in 2017 focusing on constructions of gender has such a robust and strong history upon which to build and therefore can present another portrait of gender from the vantage point of the passing of another decade. Building on previous work, this volume tackles new and extended conceptions of gender to include issues facing the lesbian, gay, bisexual, transgender, and queer (LGBTQ) community; highlights the intersections of race and gender; and addresses how gender performance (Butler, 2003) continues to influence the experiences of men and women in the 2-year college sector.

Some may question why a volume on gender in community colleges is still needed and argue that the "women's issue" in higher education is no longer a problem. But, even today, issues of gender are relevant (Eddy, Ward, & Khwaja, 2017). Though parity in numbers is evident for student enrollment and faculty representation, the glass ceiling—or as some argue the plexiglass ceiling (Glazer-Raymo, 2008) remains intact. Despite the fact that women now represent half of chief academic officers (CAO), the typical stepping-stone to the presidency, they are not advancing to the presidency in equal numbers. Part of the issue is that sitting CAOs (including both men

NEW DIRECTIONS FOR COMMUNITY COLLEGES, no. 179, Fall 2017 © 2017 Wiley Periodicals, Inc.
Published online in Wiley Online Library (wileyonlinelibrary.com) • DOI: 10.1002/cc.20257

and women), like their presidential counterparts, are at or near retirement age (ACE, 2012; Eckel, Cook, & King, 2009). The bigger issue, however, is that both men and women holding CAO positions are not considering a presidency, and the major reason (60%) given is because the work is unappealing (Eckel et al., 2009).

Yes, women are faring better in community colleges relative to their 4-year counterparts (ACE, 2012; NCES, 2013), but these statistics tell only part of the story. Historically, community colleges, as the "people's college" have been viewed as sites for inclusion for students, faculty, staff, and administrators (Townsend & Twombly, 2007). But this inclusiveness often meant that it was White women who were reaching these levels of parity rather than women of color. Faculty and leaders of color, overall, are less represented in community colleges (23% of faculty and 13% of presidents; ACE, 2012). When we complicate the idea of gender and view it in its socially constructed state versus a mere binary of men and women, other topics for consideration emerge. First, the foregone conclusion that men are by default the privileged norm ignores the fact that not all men are reaping the benefits of the system. Indeed, recent focus on masculinity, Black men, and men of color paints a more complex portrait than the foregone historic dominance by White men (Bush & Bush, 2005). Second, as a social construct, gender is represented in many forms. Research on LGBTQ populations in higher education settings expands binary reduction of gender. To date, the bulk of LGBTQ research in community colleges focuses on students (Ivory, 2005; Zamani-Gallaher & Choudhuri, 2011), and there is scant research regarding LGBTQ faculty roles and leadership in community colleges. Finally, the recent publication by Sheryl Sandberg (2013) titled *Lean In* argues that women are holding back in their aspirations and that if they just try harder, gains will be made. This argument ignores the structural issues challenging women—and men as they seek work–family balance (Eddy & Ward, 2015, 2017).

When we reduce concerns of gender in community colleges to White women, we miss the opportunity to understand more fully the broader manifestation of gender and how individuals are affected by structural constraints. Butler (2003) discussed the role of gender performance in which individuals get rewarded for acting within their "gender" and punished when acting outside these gender norms. This volume intends to challenge these historic concepts of gender performance and highlight how gender is much wider in its application and influence on campus already. What continues to be needed are changes in 2-year college culture to offer true inclusivity. When we get to this point, community colleges will truly be the people's colleges for *all* people.

The first portion of this volume discusses the ways in which structures and policies promote or challenge women seeking advancement. Chapter 1 by Jaime Lester and Carrie Klein sets the stage for the volume by providing an overview of the status of women in community colleges. They underscore how institutional structures and policies reinforce larger societal beliefs about the work that have prescribed expectations for women and men, but they note how the community colleges also can and do work toward equity. Yet, inequities persist. Lester and Klein highlight how gender performance dictates particular types of exhibition of masculinity, particularly for men of color. The authors offer several suggestions for ways to change practices on campus to achieve more inclusivity.

Amy Edwards presents in Chapter 2 a review of women in leadership in community colleges. Here, she focuses in particular on the role of communication in leadership. Findings highlight evidence of gendered communication and also the performance of gender by women leaders that is reified by physical appearance. Another challenge faced by the women leaders included in the research Edwards conducted were issues of pay equity. Chapter 3, by Rosemary Gillett-Karam, continues the focus on gender and leadership. She provides a detailed history of the evolution of women and leadership in the community college and reports on data collected from 30 participants, including administrators, board members, and presidents. Gillett-Karam found that efforts to improve gender parity in leadership are aided by the narratives of successful leadership. Leaders who see leadership as learning (Amey, 2013) are able to frame their leadership differently and create positive meaning for campus stakeholders. But, in order for leaders to be effective on campus, they must first be hired for the job. Gillett-Karam found that proactive board hires to promote gender equity are essential to obtaining more inclusive leadership in community colleges.

In Chapter 4, using 15 years of longitudinal data, Kelly Ward and Lisa Wolf-Wendel report on how women community college faculty juggle work and family. A robust long-term inquiry into the reality of academic career pathways provides insights into what best supports women and how they see their experiences. Ward and Wolf-Wendel found that their participants had intentionality in choosing the community college as a place of work given the flexibility it provided for balance. Over time, however, women noted a decreased desire to seek top-level leadership positions, citing bureaucracy and a satisfaction with their current positions based on the flexibility afforded by not moving up. A question that emerges from this research is whether community colleges act to cool women's intentions to move to senior leadership positions.

Ashleigh Lee reviews the evolution of the Cleary Act since its inception in 1990 to the present day in chapter 5. This legislation requires colleges to report statistics on various criminal activities occurring on campus. Recent focus on sexual assaults occurring on college campuses spurred public demands for attention to this problem, and other safety issues, facing college students. Because women and LGBTQ students are most often victims of sexual assault on campus, the ways in which we think about constructions of gender and how in turn we define gender are critical to the creation of policy and procedures on campus.

NEW DIRECTIONS FOR COMMUNITY COLLEGES • DOI: 10.1002/cc

The next set of chapters reviews the experiences of specific groups in community colleges to determine how they construct their gender identity. It is at the point of intersection that multiple identities connect and interact but are often not accounted for in conversations on various campus roles. Specifically, Chapter 6 by Dawn Person, Robert Dawson, Yvonne García, and Andrew Jones, focuses on the intersection of race and gender for men of color. The authors cull data from three different studies that allow for a multiple perspective analysis of the issue. This chapter highlights the evolution of masculinity studies over the past decade. Because community colleges enroll the largest numbers of minority men (NCES, 2013), it is important to understand what supports their success. Findings from the research by these authors suggest that despite challenges at the college (e.g., finances, academics) and outside of the college (e.g., family, work) that men participating in the three projects reported they had strong desires to be successful and drew on internal resiliency and support via engagement on campus with others and through student organizations and programs. A set of best practices are identified to help better support men of color in community colleges.

Chapter 7, by Judie Heineman, also deals with intersecting identities. In this case, Heineman studied the experiences of women veterans. She found specific differences between the experiences of the women veterans compared to what is known of the experiences of male veterans. "Despite only making up 10 percent to 12 percent of military personnel, women make up 27 percent of veterans enrolled in post-secondary education" (National Conference of State Legislatures, 2014, para. 4). The women participants in Heineman's study reported on how their gendered military experiences influenced how they interacted with veteran support services on campus, as they typically did not access this resource. Instead, the women veterans took a more individualized and self-focused approach to their transition to being a student–veteran. Heightened awareness of ways to best support this population is provided.

Another group that experiences intersections of gender construction is LGBTQ students. In Chapter 8, Eboni Zamani-Gallaher discusses the fluid nature of gender development for these students. She explores the privilege afforded to cisgender students and how the community college climate influences the student experience. Because the college years are a time of exploration and development of identity, LGBTQ students often run into challenges if their community college does not have a progressive system in place that allows for a range of gender expression or gender identity, including preferred name and pronoun use. Yet, the biggest conclusion of this chapter is how much remains unknown about the LGBTQ student experience in community colleges.

The final chapter of the volume, Chapter 9 by Pamela Eddy, reviews emerging trends regarding the construction of gender in community colleges and provides a summary of areas for future research. Critically, strategies are provided for individuals, leaders, and boards of trustees on ways to create a more gender-inclusive 2-year sector. As evident throughout the chapters in this volume, not all changes will occur through individual action given the role and sway of structures, norms, and policies in place. A key start to change is questioning these unseen assumptions and norms and continuing to ask a central question—why?

Leaders in community colleges and researchers can use these chapters as information sources to help guide consideration of the role of gender in institutional policies, governance, student and faculty experiences, and leadership. Individuals holding a range of roles covered in this volume will find sources of identification for shared experiences and importantly understanding for experiences of gender outside of their own. The intention of this volume is to reinforce the complexities inherent in discussion of gender in community colleges and to encourage more sustainable ways to increase inclusivity to help secure equity for all.

Pamela L. Eddy
Editor

References

American Council on Education. (1986). *The American college president*. Washington, DC: Author.

American Council on Education. (2012). *The American college president: 2012*. Washington, DC: Author.

Amey, M. J. (2013). Leadership: Community college transitions. In J. S. Levin & S. T. Kater (Eds.), *Understanding community colleges* (pp. 135–152). New York, NY: Routledge.

Bush, E. C., & Bush, L. (2005). Black male achievement and the community college. *Black Issues in Higher Education*, 22(2), 44.

Butler, J. (2003). Performative acts and gender constitution. In P. Auslander (Ed.), *Performance: Critical concepts in literary and cultural studies* (pp. 97–110). New York, NY: Routledge.

Eckel, P. D., Cook, B. J., & King, J. E. (2009). *The CAO census: A national profile of chief academic officers*. Washington, DC: American Council on Education.

Eddy, P. L., & Ward, K. (2015). *Lean In* or opt out? Career pathways of academic women. *Change*, 47(2), 16–22.

Eddy, P. L., & Ward, K. (2017). Problematizing gender in higher education: Why *Leaning In* isn't enough. In P. L. Eddy, K. Ward, & T. Khwaja (Eds.), *Critical approaches to women and gender in higher education* (pp. 13–29). New York, NY: Palgrave.

Eddy, P. L., Ward, K., & Khwaja, T. (Eds.). (2017). *Critical approaches to women and gender in higher education*. New York, NY: Palgrave.

Glazer-Raymo, J. (2008). *Unfinished agendas: New and continuing gender challenges in higher education*. Baltimore, MD: Johns Hopkins University.

Ivory, B. T. (2005). LGBT students in community college: Characteristics, challenges, and recommendations. In R. L. Sanlo (Ed.), *New Directions for Student Services: No. 111. Gender identity and sexual orientation: Research, policy, and personal* (pp. 61–69). San Francisco, CA: Jossey-Bass.

Lester, J. (Ed.). (2008). *New Directions for Community Colleges: No. 142. Gendered perspectives on community college.* San Francisco, CA: Jossey-Bass.
National Conference of State Legislatures. (2014). *Veterans in college.* Washington, DC: Author. Retrieved from http://www.ncsl.org/research/education/veterans-and-college.aspx#_ednref2
National Council on Education Statistics. (2013). *Digest of education statistics.* Washington, DC: Author.
Sandberg, S. (2013). *Lean in: Women, work, and the will to lead.* New York, NY: Knopf.
Townsend, B. (Ed.). (1995). *New Directions for Community Colleges: No. 89. Gender and power in the community college.* San Francisco, CA: Jossey-Bass.
Townsend, B. K., & Twombly, S. B. (2007). Accidental equity: The status of women in the community college. *Equity & Excellence in Education, 40*(3), 208–217.
Zamani-Gallaher, E. M., & Choudhuri, D. D. (2011). A primer on LGBTQ students at community colleges: Considerations for research and practice. In E. M. Cox & J. S. Watson (Eds.), *New Directions for Community Colleges: No. 155. Marginalized students* (pp. 35–49). San Francisco, CA: Jossey-Bass.

PAMELA L. EDDY is a professor of higher education and department chair of Educational Policy, Planning, and Leadership at the College of William & Mary. Her research focuses on community college leadership, gender, and faculty development.

1

This chapter provides a portrait of the overrepresentation of women in community colleges and introduces contemporary research on men and masculinity to argue the need for more inclusive conceptualizations of gender issues.

Setting the Stage: Broadly Considering Gender Constructions

Jaime Lester, Carrie Klein

In 2008, I, Jaime, had the pleasure of editing a volume of *New Directions for Community Colleges* titled, "Gender Perspectives on Community College." The intent of that volume was to broaden the discussion of gender in community colleges to introduce new work related to men and masculinity, noninstructional staff, work–life balance, and women in science and engineering. The chapter authors laid out a complex interplay between gender, identity, organizational dynamics, and policy that often work in concert, although not intentionally, to create an environment that creates or supports structures that prevent gender equity. Importantly, many institutional structures and practices are not intended to create gender inequity (e.g., standardized hours, hiring practices, family, and medical leave benefits) but are representations and symptoms of the greater sociological beliefs and practices pervading American society, which are predicated upon the "ideal worker"[1] (Williams, 2000, p. 2). Yet, as the 2008 volume concluded, community colleges can and do work toward equity, because they are institutions built to support open access and to serve those who are often marginalized in American society.

Fast forwarding to 2017, the purpose of this chapter is to engage recent research on women in community colleges and to broaden our collective understanding of how and why gender inequity continues. We begin with a presentation of the status of women in community colleges to highlight where gender inequities persist, despite an overall increase in the number of women in community colleges. Following is a review of the contemporary research on gender related to men and masculinity, identity, the intersection of multiple identities, and work–life balance. Each of these areas highlights the complex nature of how gender operates in organizations, specifically

New Directions for Community Colleges, no. 179, Fall 2017 © 2017 Wiley Periodicals, Inc.
Published online in Wiley Online Library (wileyonlinelibrary.com) • DOI: 10.1002/cc.20258

community colleges. The intent of these foci is to provide detailed recommendations for intervention to either uncover or give name to inequities or to provide concrete means for addressing those inequities. In the spirit of gender and organization scholars such as Rosabeth Moss Kanter (1977), Joan Williams (1989, 2000), and Joan Acker (1990, 1992), calling attention to how organizations are gendered and how the processes (policies, practices, and cultural norms) themselves create gender inequities, provide an opportunity for change.

Status of Women in Community Colleges

In fall 2014, community colleges made up 39% of undergraduate enrollment (6.7 million students) (National Center for Education Statistics [NCES], 2016a). Between 2014 and 2025, enrollment at 2-year institutions is projected to increase by 21% to 8.2 million students, whereas enrollment at 4-year institutions is projected to increase by 10% to 11.6 million students (NCES, 2016b). Given the numbers of students enrolling in courses at community colleges, these institutions are a significant option for individuals seeking a college education and, consequently, an important site to examine and to promote gender equity.

As of 2014, 3.82 million, or 57%, of community college enrollees were women (American Association of Community Colleges [AACC], 2016; NCES, 2015). Historically, women have outpaced men in enrollments in community colleges due to the flexibility in part-time schedules, access to vocational education, and location near communities, families, and workplaces (American Association of University Women [AAUW], 2013; Radford & Tasoff, 2009). Generally, the community college provides women who are seeking affordable higher education an option for them to balance their responsibilities—whether these be parents, children, communities, or employment. Women are not only enrolled in community colleges at higher rates than men, but they also are in the majority across ethnic groups. Women have outpaced men in completion rates at the community college too (typically 60% and higher; NCES, 2012). These increasing degree attainments correlate with increased earnings for women, who, when attaining an associate's degree earn on average 22% more in earnings compared to those with only a high school diploma (versus 13% for male associate degree completers; AAUW, 2013, p. 15).

Although women do tend to enroll in and complete college at rates greater than men, both at community colleges and universities, looking at degrees earned in the aggregate is misleading. Women are typically segregated into lower paying academic disciplines and degrees (AAUW, 2013). A 2011 report by the Georgetown University Center for Education and the Workforce (GUCEW) found that women and those in historically underrepresented groups typically cluster into lower paying degrees of study and fields, and even when women went into majors or fields that led to higher paying fields, they were typically paid 30% less than males. Further, when fields start accepting greater numbers of women, the associated pay with jobs in those fields begins to decline (GUCEW, 2011).

In addition to inequitable outcomes, women often also face campus climates that can affect their success. "Chilly classroom climates" at community colleges can have a negative impact on cognitive outcomes for women (Pascarella et al., 1997, p. 109; Whitt, Pascarella, Nora, & Terenzini, 1999, p. 163). These climates create an environment in which women are marginalized through stereotyping, bias, and other "inhospitable" actions by their faculty, administrators, or fellow students (Pascarella et al., 1997, p. 110). Consequently, despite women being the majority of students enrolled in community colleges and earning a majority of degrees and credentials on those campuses, they are more likely to be negatively affected by perceived and actual inequities than their male counterparts.

Evidence of Other Gender Inequities

The statistics on women in community colleges identify clear inequities, despite decades of attention and some programmatic and interventionist efforts to create more gender parity. Questions continue as to why women are not making progress, and recent questions are expanding conversations of gender beyond simply women. For example, researchers are examining the relationship between the representation of men of color in community colleges and masculinity (Harris & Wood, 2013; Sáenz, Mayo, Miller, & Rodriguez, 2015; Urias & Wood, 2015), the role of gender and social norms (Eddy & Cox, 2008; Eddy & VanDerLinden, 2006; Gill & Jones, 2013; Madden, 2011), and the impact of work–life policies (Eddy, Ward, & Khwaja, 2017; Wood, Harrison, & Jones, 2016). Essentially, the landscape of gender inequity in community colleges has significantly broadened to include men, race, ethnicity, masculinity, performance, LGBTQ populations, and agency. Agency is manifested in the ways individuals exist and act within and in reaction to the context of community college organizational power structures.

Men of Color.   The research on gender in community colleges has been significantly deepened by a focus on the success of men of color. Driven by high enrollment numbers but low college completion rates of Black and Latino men, scholars have developed a strong research portfolio with a focus on the relationship between gender, race, and identity (Harris & Wood, 2013; Sáenz et al., 2015; Urias & Wood, 2015; Wood et al., 2016). Men of color are more likely than Whites to enroll in community college and at disproportionality higher rates (Sáenz & Ponjuan, 2011). The majority of Black men in higher education are enrolled in community colleges (63.2%; National Postsecondary Student Aid Study, 2012), and the enrollment for Latino males has increased (Sáenz et al., 2015). Reasons cited in the literature for the predominance of men of color at community colleges include affordability of 2-year colleges; availability of part-time and evening course schedules; availability of vocational certificates; and the ability to attend college near families (Fry, 2002). These reasons align with the demographic characteristics of Black men in community colleges, who are more likely to be older, married, attend college part time, and have children or dependents (Wood & Williams, 2013). College completion is disproportionality low for men of color. Latino male retention rates, for example, are less than 50% 6 years after initial enrollment (Urias & Wood, 2015) and 13%–25.6% of Black males complete and/or transfer from community college within 3 years (Wood & Newman, 2015). Disaggregated data highlight aspects of gender inequities that move beyond binary disparities and toward a complex understanding of the interplay between gender, race, ethnicity, and identity. This perspective complicates the previous research, which assumed research on gender was research on women and on research that focused on 4-year versus community college experiences.

Although there remain barriers to retention and timely completion for men of color, generally, there are also data on the factors that contribute to their success (although these factors are often complicated within the specific context of community colleges). Harris and Wood (2013) provide a conceptual model on student success factors for Black men at 4-year universities, which includes five domains: academic, environmental, noncognitive, institutional, and social. Within this model, the success of Black men is shaped by factors found in research on college students more generally, such as precollege characteristics (age, high school grade point averages, and academic preparation), academic engagement, and participation in social activities in college. Hagedorn, Maxwell, and Hampton (2001) found that age, high school grade point averages, and educational goals contribute to Black student success at universities. Other studies also found that time spent studying, lower absenteeism, and educational goals affect success (Mason, 1998; Wood & Hilton, 2012). Sense of belonging, spending time socially engaging on campus, faculty–student interaction, and participation in campus-based programming are important factors in the success of students of color (Kuh, Kinzie, Buckley, Bridges, & Hayek, 2006; Strayhorn, 2008a, 2008b).

Whereas the research of men of color at 4-year universities provides data on the distinct factors for success, similar research done at the community college level offers new insight that, at times, challenges the conventions of significant factors to college student success. Often, these factors are directly related to race, perceptions of racism, and cultural notions of masculinity. For example, Sutherland (2011) found that men of color in community colleges experience "social incongruence," often feeling as outsiders on campus (p. 275). These feelings were derived from direct experience with faculty and staff representing the campuses. Gardenshire-Crooks, Collado, Martin, and Castro (2010) noted similar findings attributing the outsider perception to students' experience of racism and racial prejudice.

Several other studies have identified an important nuance to the long-held assumption that more academic integration leads to greater college student success. On average and across multiple studies (Bush & Bush, 2010; Wood & Turner, 2010), Black men tend to be less academically integrated compared to their peers; yet, paradoxically, studies also indicate that integration can have a negative effect (Wood, 2012) or that more integration can actually lead to less satisfaction (Strayhorn, 2012). Experience of racial prejudice creates a negative association with increased engagement on campus, prompting students to shy away from further integration. Other studies have shown that Black men need to increase faculty–student interactions but are often reluctant to engage because of fears of being viewed as academically incapable or less prepared (Wood, 2014).

Gender Performance and Masculinity.   Research on gender performance has gained traction. Framing gender more as an expression of identity (rather than biology) and of social and cultural norms, scholars have revealed the relationship between gendered behavior and success for students and faculty. Harris (2008) applied Kimmel and Messner's (2007) masculinity perspective to men in 4-year universities finding that men performed in stereotypical masculine ways to receive validation from their peers. Those behaviors included homophobia, treating women disrespectfully, and drinking alcohol excessively.

Sáenz, Bukoski, Lu, and Rodriguez (2013) have conducted multiple studies on the role of masculinity among Latino men. Drawing on the work of male gender role conflict (O'Neil, 1981) and machismo, which is defined as socially expected behaviors that are aggressive and denote power and control, Sáenz and colleagues (2013) have illuminated the complex and oftentimes contradictory nature of machismo and Latino student success. Referred to as "quasipositive," they found that the competition and pride associated with masculinity benefitted those who were academically successful but demotivated those male students who were less successful (Sáenz et al., 2013, p. 89). Machismo motivated the Latino students to try harder and to compete academically but also led to a lack of help-seeking behaviors, as the expectation is that men should not fail, nor should they need help. Spurred by this thinking, students would also forgo the development of supportive peer groups within the community college context (Sáenz et al., 2013). A similar study revealed a relationship between employment, social status, and masculinity. The masculine expectation to provide financially for one's family drew Latino males away from college and into full-time employment. As Sáenz and colleagues concluded, "this strain presses on cultural beliefs that men must financially support themselves and their families, and peers from outside the community college context do not necessarily identify higher education as a means to support one's family" (2015, p. 173). These contradictions underscore the impact of the multifaceted nature of gender performance.

The paradoxes found in gender performance are not germane just to students. Lester (2008) in a study of female community college faculty identified a similar contradiction termed hyperperformance. The participants in her study often overemphasized their gender in order to adhere to the cultural, gendered expectations inherent in their environmental circumstance, whether it be a classroom or faculty meeting.

Gender and Leadership

The endemic gender inequities present in higher education extend from students to college leadership as well. Community colleges, like traditional 4-year institutions, are influenced by the "great man" or "hero leader" narratives of leadership (Amey & Twombly, 1992; Eddy & VanDerLinden, 2006; Townsend & Twombly, 2007). This narrative has shaped ideas about what "good" leaders look like and typically include more male or masculine (and typically White male and masculine) attributes, including agentic and autocratic decision making, task and outcome orientation, and power-driven perspectives (Madden, 2011). Conversely, female-oriented leadership traits are more communally focused on shared and processual decision making (Madden, 2011). Perceptions of female-oriented leadership have evolved from the male-dominated discourse and are often viewed as less effective means for leading successful institutions (Eddy & Cox, 2008).

These narratives shape women's approaches to leadership on campus. Women in higher education find that they have to "work twice as hard to achieve the same goals" (Gill & Jones, 2013, p. 50). The need to work twice as hard is based on both a chilly campus climate that negatively affects women's ability to move ahead in leadership positions (Madsen, Longman, & Daniels, 2012; White, 2012) and gender expectations. Women often find themselves in a double bind—constrained by traditional notions of who leaders should be (male) and by perceptions of how they should engage in leadership (ideal worker). Women are often criticized for their choices to engage in more male-oriented leadership to get ahead in male-oriented institutions yet also criticized for more feminized ways of being (Gill & Jones, 2013; Madden, 2011; Madsen et al., 2012). Male-oriented leadership is often associated with instrumentalist leadership styles that focus on tasks and outcomes versus the relational style associated with female-oriented leadership, which focuses on processes and persons (Gill & Jones, 2013; Vanderslice & Litsch, 1998).

Madden (2011) argued that the "masculinized and bureaucratic" hierarchies act as a significant barrier to women advancing in higher education (p. 64). The challenge with these hierarchical structures is that they require "autocratic, self-promoting, competitive behavior, all of which are viewed negatively when engaged by women" (Madden, 2011, p. 66). For women of color, the impact is twofold. Women leaders of color often have to deal with both sexism and racism and their presence decreases as rank increases. Further, fewer opportunities for socialization and professional development, which minimizes future opportunities (Madden, 2011).

Because leadership is shaped by these narratives, ascending to upper levels of leadership is particularly difficult for women. Consequently, although women make up the majority of positions in community colleges (and at higher rates than in traditional 4-year institutions) and are "well-represented in midlevel positions," they are "underrepresented in senior-level positions" (Townsend & Twombly, 2007, p. 281). As of 2012, women made up 33% of community college presidencies (American Council on Education [ACE], 2012). As older community college leaders are retiring, numbers of women in the upper levels of management are increasing, a trend that is likely to continue (ACE, 2012; Eddy & VanDerLinden, 2006). These women are often mentored by men with traditional male leadership attributes, so they will often default to more masculine ways of being as they relate to leadership (Madden, 2011). However, the "feminine" characteristics of leadership may be just what the increasingly flat organizational structures of community colleges need. For example, Gill and Jones (2013) argued that based on recent studies, the "leadership traits often attributed to women have shaped the direction of administration in community colleges" (p. 49). For leadership change to take place, increasing the numbers of women in power is not enough. Leaders at all levels of community colleges, male and female, must understand the mission and needs of community colleges and the advantages that "feminine" leadership attributes, specifically shared leadership and inclusive decision making, can have for their organizations as they work to mitigate the challenges facing higher education.

Implications for Practice

Knowledge regarding gender equity in community colleges continues to deepen and broaden with more insight into the experiences of gender across identities, expression of gender performance, and the relationship of gender with power and agency. Even though this knowledge may seem esoteric and theoretical at times, there are important actionable implications for individuals and teams working in community colleges.

- *Disaggregate data by gender, gender identities, and race/ethnicity.* Inspired by the Equity Scorecard Project (University of Southern California, 2016), data analysis on student progress and success needs to include more refinement to account for differences by gender and race/ethnicity and other identity groups. All too often, campuses report on the success of students in the aggregate, such as simple percentages of completion; however, disaggregating data by student gender and identity groups provides an opportunity for organizational learning and the potential for interventions that address the specific needs of those groups.

New Directions for Community Colleges • DOI: 10.1002/cc

- *Work to create a climate of inclusivity and to address gender disparities.* Institutions should look to improve the campus climate as it relates to gender, gender identities, and race/ethnicity. Resources like the Campus Pride Index (www.campusprideindex.org) provide benchmarking for institutions that seek to improve their climates as they relate to gender and identity-based disparities. Recent literature on microaggressions, for example, reveals that individual experience with racism and other forms of microaggressions influences overall perceptions of campus climate and a student's sense of belonging (McCabe, 2009; Solórzano, Ceja, & Yosso, 2000; Yosso, Smith, Ceja, & Solórzano, 2007).
- *Critically examine campus symbols and artifacts for gendering.* Critically viewing campus policies and statements is especially important (Allan, Iverson, & Ropers-Huilman, 2009). Nondiscrimination clauses and anti-harassment statements should be inclusive of all gender expressions and work to protect all members of the campus community. Further, actual symbols and spaces, like university forms, bathroom signs, and campus facilities, should support inclusivity. The American Council on Education's (2013) *A Matter of Excellence: Guide to Strategic Diversity Leadership and Accountability in Higher Education* recommends the creation of diversity definitions and working terminology to conceptualize those definitions.
- *Provide cultural integration and training.* Wood and Hilton (2012) found that spirituality had an impact on African American student success by providing meaning and purpose, reducing feelings of isolation, and fostering a focus on academic excellence. Attention should be paid to training and developing faculty and staff to address issues of inequities on campus and to work to establish a climate of inclusivity and support for women and students from historically underrepresented groups. Further professional development of leadership should include an understanding of how women come to leadership positions in a way that may be different from the way men do (Madsen et al., 2012).
- *Think critically to improve and create pipelines.* Marybeth Gasman (2016) argued that instead of complaining about pipeline issues, campus leaders should work actively and collectively to build pathways that "encourage, mentor, and support people of color" (p. 1) and to critically reflect on their roles as they relate to encouraging the status quo versus pushing for needed change. Simply stating that it is difficult to address disparities by race/ethnicity and other groups does not even begin to develop interventions, question organizational practices, and alleviate those inequities. The first step of disaggregating data by gender, race/ethnicity, and other underrepresented groups identifies where inequities in retention and outcomes lie, but it must be followed with intensive discussion with students to identify why those disparities persist.

Conclusion

Community colleges have historically been places of opportunity. The structure, access, and affordability of these institutions have made them particularly appealing places for women and students from historically underrepresented or marginalized groups to pursue higher education. Despite the success of these institutions, community colleges need to do more to understand and address the inherent and inherited inequities to better serve their students and to better meet their missions. The remaining chapters in this volume help highlight a range of opportunities to change community colleges to become more inclusive.

Note

1. "The ideal worker is someone who works at least forty hours a week year-round. This ideal-worker norm, framed around the traditional life patterns of men, excludes most mothers of childbearing age" (Williams, 2000, p. 2).

References

Acker, J. (1990). Hierarchies, jobs, bodies: A theory of gendered organizations. *Gender & Society, 4*, 139–158.

Acker, J. (1992). From sex roles to gendered institutions. *Contemporary Sociology, 21*, 565–569.

Allan, E., Iverson, S. V., & Ropers-Huilman, R. (2009). *Reconstructing policy in higher education: Feminist poststructural perspectives.* New York, NY: Routledge.

American Association of Community Colleges. (2016). *2016 fast facts.* Retrieved from http://www.aacc.nche.edu/AboutCC/Documents/AACCFactSheetsR2.pdf

American Association of University Women. (2013). *Women in community colleges: Access to success.* Retrieved from http://www.aauw.org/resource/women-in-community-colleges/

American Council on Education. (2012). *The American college president: 2012.* Washington, DC: Author.

American Council on Education. (2013). *A matter of excellence: A guide to strategic diversity leadership and accountability in higher education.* Washington, DC: Author.

Amey, M. J., & Twombly, S. B. (1992). Re-visioning leadership in community colleges. *Review of Higher Education, 15*, 125–150.

Bush, E. C., & Bush, L. (2010). Calling out the elephant: An examination of African American male achievement in community colleges. *Journal of African American Males in Education, 1*(1), 40–62.

Eddy, P. L., & Cox, E. M. (2008). Gendered leadership: An organizational perspective. In J. Lester (Ed.), *New Directions for Community Colleges: No. 142. Gendered perspectives on community colleges* (pp. 69–79). San Francisco, CA: Jossey-Bass.

Eddy, P. L., & VanDerLinden, K. E. (2006). Emerging definitions of leadership in higher education: New visions of leadership or same old "hero" leader? *Community College Review, 34*(1), 5–26.

Eddy, P. L., Ward, K., & Khwaja, T. (2017). *Critical approaches to women and gender in higher education.* New York, NY: Palgrave Macmillan.

Fry, R. (2002). *Latinos in higher education: Many enroll, too few graduate*. Washington, DC: Pew Hispanic Center. Retrieved from http://files.eric.ed.gov/fulltext/ED468848.pdf

Gardenshire-Crooks, A., Collado, H., Martin, K., & Castro, A. (2010). *Terms of engagement: Men of color discuss their experiences in community college*. New York, NY: MDRC. Retrieved from http://files.eric.ed.gov/fulltext/ED508982.pdf

Gasman, M. (2016). Here are the excuses I hear about why colleges don't hire more faculty of color. *Linked In*. Retrieved from https://www.linkedin.com/pulse/heres-what-one-tell-you-why-colleges-dont-hire-more-faculty-gasman?trk=hp-feed-article-title-share

Georgetown University Center on Education and the Workforce. (2011, Nov.). *Career clusters: Forecasting demand for high school through college jobs*. Washington, DC: Author. Retrieved from https://cew.georgetown.edu/wp-content/uploads/2014/11/clusters-complete-update1-1.pdf

Gill, K., & Jones, S. J. (2013). Fitting in: Community college female executive leaders share their experiences—A study in West Texas. *NASPA Journal About Women in Higher Education, 6*(1), 48–70.

Hagedorn, L. S., Maxwell, W., & Hampton, P. (2001). Correlates of retention for African-American males in community colleges. *Journal of College Student Retention: Research, Theory & Practice, 3*, 243–263.

Harris, F., III (2008). Deconstructing masculinity: A qualitative study of college men's masculine conceptualizations and gender performance. *NASPA Journal, 45*, 453–474.

Harris, F., III, & Wood, J. L. (2013). Student success for men of color in community colleges: A review of published literature and research, 1998–2012. *Journal of Diversity in Higher Education, 6*, 174–185.

Kanter, R. M. (1977). *Men and women of the corporation*. New York, NY: Basic Books.

Kimmel, M. S., & Messner, M. A. (2007). Men as gendered beings. In *Men's lives*. New York, NY: Pearson.

Kuh, G. D., Kinzie, J., Buckley, J. A., Bridges, B. K., & Hayek, J. C. (2006, July). *What matters to student success: A review of the literature*. Commissioned report for the National Symposium on Postsecondary Student Success: Spearheading a dialog on student success. Washington, DC: National Postsecondary Education Cooperative.

Lester, J. (2008). Performing gender in the workplace gender socialization, power, and identity among women faculty members. *Community College Review, 35*, 277–305.

Madden, M. (2011). Gender stereotypes of leaders: Do they influence leadership in higher education? *Wagadu: A Journal of Transnational Women's and Gender Studies, 9*, 55–88.

Madsen, S. R., Longman, K. A., & Daniels, J. R. (2012). Women's leadership development in higher education: Conclusion and implications for HRD. *Advances in Developing Human Resources, 14*(1), 113–128.

Mason, H. P. (1998). A persistence model for African American male urban community college students. *Community College Journal of Research and Practice, 22*, 751–760.

McCabe, J. (2009). Racial and gender microaggressions on a predominantly-White campus: Experiences of Black, Latina/o and White undergraduates. *Race, Gender & Class, 16*, 133–151.

National Center for Education Statistics. (2012). *Degrees conferred by race and sex*. Washington, DC: Author. Retrieved from https://nces.ed.gov/fastfacts/display.asp?id=72

National Center for Education Statistics. (2015). *Table 303.70*. Washington, DC: Author. Retrieved from http://nces.ed.gov/programs/digest/d15/tables/dt15_303.70.asp

National Center for Education Statistics. (2016a). *Digest of education statistics*. Washington, DC: Author. Retrieved from http://nces.ed.gov/programs/coe/indicator_csb.asp

National Center for Education Statistics. (2016b). *Undergraduate enrollment*. Washington, DC: Author. Retrieved from http://nces.ed.gov/programs/coe/indicator_cha.asp

National Postsecondary Student Aid Study. (2012). *NPSAS institution level by race/ethnicity (with multiple) and gender, for NPSAS institution sector (4 with multiple) (Public 2-year)*. Washington, DC: National Center for Education Statistics.

O'Neil, J. M. (1981). Patterns of gender role conflict and strain: Sexism and fear of femininity in men's lives. *Personnel & Guidance Journal, 60*, 203–211.

Pascarella, E. T., Whitt, E. J., Edison, M. I., Nora, A., Hagedorn, L. S., Yeager, P. M., & Terenzini, P. T. (1997). Women's perceptions of a "chilly climate" and their cognitive outcomes during the first year of college. *Journal of College Student Development, 38*(2), 109–124.

Radford, A. W., & Tasoff, S. (2009). *Choosing a postsecondary institution: Considerations reported by students* (NCES Report No. 2009-186). Washington, DC: National Center for Education Statistics.

Sáenz, V. B., Bukoski, B. E., Lu, C., & Rodriguez, S. (2013). Latino males in Texas community colleges: A phenomenological study of masculinity constructs and their effect on college experiences. *Journal of African American Males in Education, 4*(2), 82–102.

Sáenz, V. B., Mayo, J. R., Miller, R. A., & Rodriguez, S. L. (2015). (Re) defining masculinity through peer interactions: Latino men in Texas community colleges. *Journal of Student Affairs Research and Practice, 52*, 164–175.

Sáenz, V. B., & Ponjuan, L. (2011). *Men of color: Ensuring the academic success of Latino males in higher education*. Washington, DC: Institute for Higher Education Policy.

Solórzano, D., Ceja, M., & Yosso, T. (2000). Critical race theory, racial microaggressions, and campus racial climate: The experiences of African American college students. *Journal of Negro Education, 69*, 60–73.

Strayhorn, T. L. (2008a). Sentido de pertenencia: A hierarchical analysis predicting sense of belonging among Latino college students. *Journal of Hispanic Higher Education, 7*, 301–320.

Strayhorn, T. L. (2008b). Fittin' in: Do diverse interactions with peers affect sense of belonging for Black men at predominantly White institutions? *NASPA Journal, 45*, 501–527.

Strayhorn, T. L. (2012). Satisfaction and retention among African American men at two-year community colleges. *Community College Journal of Research and Practice, 36*, 358–375.

Sutherland, J. A. (2011). Building an academic nation through social networks: Black immigrant men in community colleges. *Community College Journal of Research and Practice, 35*, 267–279.

Townsend, B. K., & Twombly, S. B. (2007). Accidental equity: The status of women in the community college. *Equity & Excellence in Education, 40*(3), 208–217.

University of Southern California. (2016). *Equity scorecard project*. Los Angeles: Center for Urban Education. Retrieved from https://cue.usc.edu/tools/the-equity-scorecard/

Urias, M. V., & Wood, J. L. (2015). The effect of non-cognitive outcomes on perceptions of school as a feminine domain among Latino men in community college. *Culture, Society and Masculinities, 7*(1), 22–32.

Vanderslice, R., & Litsch, K. (1998). *Women in development: Advancing women in higher education* (Opinion papers, 120). (ERIC Document Reproduction Service No. ED444421).

White, J. S. (2012). HERS institutes: Curriculum for advancing women leaders in higher education. *Advances in Developing Human Resources, 14*, 11–27.

Whitt, E. J., Pascarella, E. T., Nora, A., & Terenzini, P. T. (1999). Women's perceptions of a "chilly climate" and cognitive outcomes in college: Additional evidence. *Journal of College Student Development, 40*(2), 163–177.

Williams, J. (1989). Deconstructing gender. *Michigan Law Review, 87*, 797–845.

Williams, J. (2000). *Unbending gender: Why family and work conflict and what to do about it*. New York, NY: Oxford University Press.

Wood, J. L. (2012). Black males in the community college: Using two national datasets to examine academic and social integration. *Journal of Black Masculinity*, 2(2), 56–88.

Wood, J. L. (2014). Apprehension to engagement in the classroom: Perceptions of Black males in the community college. *International Journal of Qualitative Studies in Education*, 27, 785–803.

Wood, J. L., Harrison, J. D., & Jones, T. K. (2016). Black males' perceptions of the work–college balance: the impact of employment on academic success in the community college. *Journal of Men's Studies*, 243, 326–343.

Wood, J. L., & Hilton, A. A. (2012). Spirituality and academic success: Perceptions of African American males in the community college. *Religion & Education*, 39(1), 28–47.

Wood, J. L., & Newman, C. B. (2015). Predictors of faculty–student engagement for black men in urban community colleges: An investigation of the Community College Survey of Men. *Urban Education*, 1–23. Advanced online publication, https://doi.org/10.1177/004208591623343

Wood, J. L., & Turner, C. S. (2010). Black males and the community college: Student perspectives on faculty and academic success. *Community College Journal of Research and Practice*, 35, 135–151.

Wood, J. L., & Williams, R. C. (2013). Persistence factors for Black males in the community college: An examination of background, academic, social, and environmental variables. *Spectrum: A Journal on Black Men*, 1(2), 1–28.

Yosso, T., Smith, W., Ceja, M., & Solórzano, D. (2009). Critical race theory, racial microaggressions, and campus racial climate for Latina/o undergraduates. *Harvard Educational Review*, 79, 659–691.

JAIME LESTER *is an associate professor of higher education at George Mason University who researches organizational change, leadership, learning, and social justice issues in universities and community colleges.*

CARRIE KLEIN *is a PhD research assistant in the Higher Education Program at George Mason University whose research interests include better understanding of the impact of big data on campus, specifically in the areas of interventions, individual agency, and ethics and the intersections of organizational structure, power, and privilege.*

2

This chapter provides an action plan to help achieve gender equity by better understanding the role of gender, leadership, and communication in higher education administration.

Achieving Gender Equity for Women Leaders in Community Colleges Through Better Communication

Amy Fara Edwards

As a communication studies professor, I have spent most of my professional life trying to understand how communication shapes lives and how multiple communication concepts such as perception, language, and nonverbal cues affect patterns of work in the social world (Allen, 2011). This way of understanding identity represents social constructionism, which posits that the "self is socially constructed through various relational and linguistic processes" (Carbaugh, 1996, p. 30). Similarly, Lorber (2014), a foundational theorist of social construction of gender difference, claimed "gender is constantly created and re-created out of human interaction, out of social life, and is the texture and order of that social life" (p. 19). Thus, from the time we are born, we are learning to abide by gender roles and norms, and gender, "like culture, is a human production that depends on everyone constantly 'doing gender'" (Lorber, 2014. p. 19). The ways in which individuals construct their gender identity is ongoing, and this construction influences the ways in which they engage in leading.

Each semester, I help my students uncover and explore their own identities and support their understanding of how cultural dimensions such as gender, race, and social class affect their everyday lives. I introduce students to new concepts like gender and leadership that will shape the way they view the world. Additionally, I show students that their identities are relational and impress upon them that their communication patterns and behaviors are shaped by the social world and that, through communication, they are performing gender (Allen, 2011). West and Zimmerman (1987) argued that "doing gender" involves "complex, socially guided perceptual, interactional, and micro-political activities that cast particular pursuits as

New Directions for Community Colleges, no. 179, Fall 2017 © 2017 Wiley Periodicals, Inc.
Published online in Wiley Online Library (wileyonlinelibrary.com) • DOI: 10.1002/cc.20259

expressions of masculine and feminine 'natures'" (p. 126). They popular-ized this concept of "doing gender" in which they contend that the doing of gender "is undertaken by women and men whose competence as members of society is hostage to its production" (p. 126). Thus, being in a commu-nication studies classroom in a leadership position at a community college classroom, I turned my interest toward the college itself, how it functions, and how women use communication at all levels of higher education. I then focused on how women leaders understand their gendered behaviors, find their own voice, infuse their own style, and enhance their own commu-nication competence. Such interest led to my qualitative study of women executives in higher education.

In 1986, the typical campus president was a White male in his 50s, married with children, a Protestant, held a doctorate in education, and had served in his current leadership position for approximately 6 years (Amer-ican Council on Education [ACE], 2012). Fast forward 25 years later and the leader profile has not changed much, especially in terms of the race and ethnicity, although there has been some headway in terms of gender diversity with women now holding 33% of community college presidencies (ACE, 2012). Despite the increased representation of women in top posi-tions at 2-year colleges, the rate of increase has slowed down. Between 2006 and 2012, there was an increase of only about 4% of women in senior lead-ership positions (ACE, 2012). If women continue to increase their share of presidencies by one percentage point every 2 years, it will take approx-imately 48 years to hold half of the college presidencies (Lapovsky, 2014). This timeline to achieve gender equity in community college leadership is too long, especially when doctoral trained and qualified women are in the wings with the requisite qualifications to lead (ACE, 2012; Lapovsky, 2014; White, 2013).

To understand how gender informs leadership for women leaders in higher education, I conducted a qualitative study that examined the back-grounds and leadership experiences of community college women execu-tives (two chancellors, four presidents, and two vice-presidents) in south-ern California to better understand the communication factors that con-tributed most to their success. Further, my study sought to examine the various and significant ways that interpersonal communication factors af-fected the leadership style of women administrators in higher education. The research questions for this study were (a) What role does gender play in the leadership of former, and current, women leaders in higher education? (b) What gendered and/or cultural obstacles or barriers affect the leader-ship of women administrators? and (c) How do interpersonal communica-tion factors shape the leadership experiences of women leaders in higher education?

A rhetorical feminist perspective framed this study. Feminism "gives voice to individuals marginalized and devalued by the dominant culture and, thus, provides a more holistic understanding of the world" (Foss, Foss,

& Griffin, 1999, p. 5). Feminism offers a model for different ways of living in the world, and many feminists now expand this definition to include the elimination of oppression of people who may be seen as "the other" in our culture. According to Rakow and Wackwitz (2004), "Feminist theory in communication is developed and used by scholars to understand gender as a communicative process, with the goal of making social changes important to the well-being of women and, ultimately, everyone" (p. 450). Feminist rhetoric challenges male-dominated views and theories while giving voice to women and other muted groups in society. Thus, rhetorical feminism provided an important lens for understanding the communication behaviors and the role of gender differences in executive leadership for the study's participants. Using a rhetorical feminist perspective allowed me to emphasize and critique the subordination and/or progress of women and understand how the social construction of reality influenced and, ultimately, created notions of masculinity, femininity, and androgyny. This framework provided a powerful point of view to highlight differences in communication practices affecting women leaders in community colleges.

Approach

This research used a multiple case study methodology to illuminate the role gender plays in the leadership styles of women leaders in higher education. Further, a qualitative approach allowed the participants to acknowledge their unique higher educational executive experiences (Rossman & Rallis, 2012). Two sampling strategies, stratified purposeful and criterion sampling, were employed. These criteria were used to set boundaries and frame the research study.

The data sources included interviews conducted with the selected executives from community colleges in southern California. Several women who met the criteria were asked to participate; eight women accepted and were then interviewed in one-on-one settings. Seven of the eight women were currently serving in their executive role, and one was recently retired from her presidency. Interviewing eight women executives in community college leadership positions provided the opportunity to hear their voices and allow the women to tell their stories. I was careful to protect the anonymity of my subjects by conducting the interviews in private locations. All the women were given pseudonyms and any identifiable characteristics, such as their position or academic institution, were excluded.

Findings

The interviews highlighted that women play a significant role in community college leadership and that their approaches to communication affect their experiences in meaningful ways. As one woman exclaimed:

> I think that education, the changes that have happened in education, and the metamorphosis [of women and men] in education is because of women. Education was predominantly men for so many years, and went on so much the same for so many years. It has to be women coming in that have made the substantial changes. It's certainly opened the door for others... because we created a look of opportunity.

The overarching findings presented here explicitly relate to communication, leadership, and gender. The main finding was that the participants found communication gendered, both in terms of how they were treated and how they were judged by others. The second finding related to how they were judged by their physical appearance, and the final theme focused on pay inequities.

Gendered Communication.   First, this study found that collaborative decision making is of paramount importance to women and that they use their verbal and nonverbal communication skills during collaboration to enhance decision making in professional contexts. Ultimately, the leaders are hyperfocused on inclusion and communication. One woman stated:

> I think [it] is important that you involve people who are impacted by the decisions in talking about the issues, staying issue-focused, and searching for solutions that will work for everybody. If you force it, if you're autocratic, and force a [unilateral] decision on someone, that they had no part in it, yet it impacts them, people will find a way to get around the decision and sabotage the success.

Further, this study found that communication skills affect leadership and explored how the leaders use and rely on both their oral and written communication skills on a regular basis. Some of the women felt that they are stronger presenters, whereas others felt that their writing had the most impact on their colleagues and colleges. These women executives consistently spoke about the need to communicate clearly, and often, for their messages to be understood and their goals achieved. Such communication findings are directly linked to the gendered societal and cultural norms perpetuated. Thus, this study found that gender does, in fact, affect women's leadership in educational executive positions. Three main topics emerged regarding communication, including disparate treatment for women, socialization of women, and changes in the perception of women leaders, from the past to present day. When asked if gender affects her communication and leadership, one leader put it like this:

> I hope so... You work with who you are, and part of who I am is being a woman. I'm a mom, I'm a daughter, a wife, and all of that comes to work with me. I don't know that I think that it changes how I think, but gender is real.

NEW DIRECTIONS FOR COMMUNITY COLLEGES • DOI: 10.1002/cc

Another interviewee indicated:

> You know, many communicate with a slightly misogynist attitude—and until you say to them, "I don't think so," and you draw the line in the sand, there are instances where they are willing to walk all over you. So, I think that's an issue that women have to be prepared for [in academia]—I mean I have enough self-confidence to know that I am the college president and that this college is my responsibility, not yours, and you're not going to make that decision.

How these women defined their leadership was always through a gendered lens, which in turn affected their communication approaches.

The finding of disparate treatment manifested within the gendered communication patterns noted by the participants. Two distinct issues that recur in the literature—stereotypes and the exclusion of women—were evidenced in the communication patterns noted by the participants. Although all the women claimed that stereotypes do, in fact, still exist for women, they noted that they are now much less prevalent. Over the course of their careers, they witnessed and experienced the changes in treatment of women and discrimination. Ultimately, the data revealed that these women are experiencing less overt discrimination today. As one woman observed, "I think less stereotypes exist now. Actually, a lot less," and another woman said, "I think there used to be, you know, the notion of the Wicked Witch of the West or something, but that's not as pervasive now." Another woman said:

> Women aren't the scary witch anymore. You know, the witch, the bitch, the "you don't wanna work for her because she's gonna be too hard on you." Those were the stereotypes that were most prevalent then ... I just don't hear any kind of comments of women not "earning their positions" anymore. There's an acceptance of value. You may get [the job]. You may not ... Those comments were lingering when I was a young professional ... they're not getting the job because, "oh a woman needed to get it now," [and] you don't hear the "she slept her way to the top" comment anymore. Maybe it's elsewhere, but I haven't heard it in education in a long time.

These comments underscore the fact that women think stereotypical attitudes and behaviors have diminished over time, which changes how women communicate and how others communicate with them. These executives feel much less excluded because they are women; however, not all the participants agreed with this assessment of change. For example, sports presented a targeted aspect of everyday communication at the office for women. One woman explained:

> Well, you know, when I walk into a room ... the social milling before the meeting starts—the men are talking, and they're talking about sports. [Men]

automatically assume I don't know anything about sports because I'm a woman. I tell them I love football. We start talking about football... and [I] also love the Dodgers. That's part of the respect too. That they see you [as] more than just an administrator. That you are a whole person. But they think almost immediately, "You're a woman, you're not going to understand this." And they love to, you know, Monday-morning ask me about it like a quiz, "Am I really a fan?"

Sports historically has been a male domain, and communication around sports can create exclusionary communication practices. Communication regarding sports becomes a way for men to exert their privilege and further subjugate and dominate women by assuming they do not know anything about the subject. "Testing" a woman through follow-up queries to determine if in fact she is a "true fan" feeds into gendered stereotypes. This example highlights how women need to overprepare all the time because they know they will be challenged and tested and possibly never be accepted. Disparate treatment continues to manifest in communication for women leaders.

Physical Appearance.   One way in which "doing gender" emerges in socialization for women is regarding the need to look and act in very particular ways. The women mentioned being "inspected" more in terms of how they looked compared to their male counterparts. One woman was surprised by the reactions she got from people when she became as executive. She said, "There were associations with my looks, and not about my brains." Another executive said:

I think for women, in general, we are, especially in leadership positions, scrutinized a lot more so than male administrators. Especially in terms of physical appearance... she cannot be too short or petite, she can't be too feminine, in terms of not wearing too much makeup, or too much jewelry, or have too elaborate of a hair style, or wear clothing that's too provocative. On the other hand, she can't be too masculine looking, either, or have hair that is too short or clothes that are too plain... I think that's a problem.

These expectations of "how" to appear reinforce gendered stereotypes that are socialized at a young age. Another executive added:

I don't think people perceive women who are older, as wiser. I think people perceive men who are older as wiser, but I don't know that people look the same as [at] women, which is why I think more women dye their hair, you know, change themselves physically... so that there's an impression of, youth.

Ultimately, these comments reveal that physical appearance is still an issue for women. Women are scrutinized more for how they dress and each part of their appearance can be dissected by others, especially when they are in a position of power. What people choose to wear, and under what circumstances, creates the image they want to communicate and project, and these decisions are influenced by patterns of socialization regarding gender. How women are perceived for a leadership position is often based on the first impression communicated regarding looks. One leader said:

> [Named woman] is sabotaging herself by how ultra-thin she makes herself look: her eyelashes, and her hair, and all that is just totally undercutting herself. It's hard to take, but she'll never get past the interviewing committee until she tones it down.

The perception of accepted and socialized gender norms for women continues, with women often perpetuating the very narrow norms they are trying to escape.

Pointedly, many of the women in the study did *not* address physical appearance in anyway. This lack of acknowledgement about the socialization of norms regarding physical appearance may be due to the unquestioned aspect of what women leaders should look like, or it may reflect the lack of judgment felt by the participants compared to the past. It is important to remember that physical appearance reflects one form of nonverbal communication, and as such, women may face different norms than men do.

Pay Inequity.   Even with changing perceptions of acceptance of women as leaders, a persistent issue remains regarding inequity in salary and compensation for women relative to men. Half of the women (four of eight women) in this study mentioned this issue. The other half of the participants did not think of it, nor did they mention it, as an issue. The women who brought up pay inequity as an issue described, in detail, how the pay scale is tipped in the male executives' direction. One woman said:

> Oh, yeah, pay is an issue. I know of women who should've been rated higher, in comparison to others. I know that I argued, in terms of my rating .... And, you're okay with things until you find out that men are higher. Okay? I was surprised with two women that had leadership positions before [coming to this district] that they were not given high enough [payscale] steps .... one of them, I was kind of taken aback, that she wasn't more vocal about it. But, it's happened.

Several other instances emerged regarding concern with compensation. Because the board of trustees typically makes the decision about where employees start on the pay scale when they enter a new position and/or a new district, this decision on starting pay communicates a sense of worth. Despite the fact that the women were in senior leadership positions, evidencing changing perceptions of who can lead today's community colleges, differentials in pay highlight that changes have not occurred in all areas.

Relationships.   Other findings in this study related to a woman's relationships, both personal and professional. Socialized gender norms were evident in how the participants communicated their balance of professional roles and family responsibilities. Here, the women spoke about making career moves when the time was right for their families rather than when it was right for them. Most of the women remained very conscious of their family's needs and wanted to make their own professional moves when it would cause the least amount of turmoil in the family. The women waited for their spouse's careers to take off first, or their child's educational needs to be met first, before moving forward with their own aspirations.

Ultimately, recognizing the role of gendered communication and socialized gender norms for women may enhance the success of women leaders in higher education. To keep challenging the existing gendered norms and to push women to question these norms and to create a broader conception of how to lead with strong communication, recommendations for future practice are offered next.

Recommendations for Future Practice

Specific recommendations are offered to help challenge socialized communication norms regarding women leaders. The recommendations that follow are organized into three categories: (a) recommendations specifically for women leaders, (b) recommendations for all leaders, and (c) for future research. These recommendations have the potential to result in changes in educational policy and practice that may provide an action plan for better understanding the role of gender, leadership, and communication in higher education administration.

Recommendations for Women Leaders.   Based on the interviews conducted, this study found that although there are still very real challenges for women, being a woman in a leadership position in higher education was not perceived to be as big a hindrance compared to the past. The participants offered advice for others, such as advocating that women truly knowing themselves and make the right choices for themselves, at the right time. Many of the women leaders said things like, "Be sure an executive position is what you want," or "Know yourself, so you can make the right choice." Three specific recommendations were offered by the participants:

1. Women leaders must continue to become mentors for other women. Many of the women interviewed in this study discussed the fact that a mentor helped them make the decision to apply for an administrative job; these mentors, however, were all men. Most the women said, explicitly, that women must mentor other women, so many of the issues women face can be discussed with the tried and true knowledge and wisdom of a woman's experience. Women can speak to other women

with a real understanding of the issues women face and can help other women understand and use their communication skills.

2. Women need to continue learning and using different communicative coping mechanisms, especially in those moments that are highly stressful because of negative perceptions and stereotypes perpetuated throughout history. Based on the results of this study, women leaders do, in fact, deal with more sexism and more inappropriate behaviors from others. Women need to continue to develop self-esteem, self-confidence, and inner strength to better deal with people and problems as changes continue regarding the perceptions of what it means to be a woman leader. As the women from this study suggested, women leaders need to communicate clearly, accurately, and with confidence while remaining cool headed and rational to deal with the more personal side of the job.

3. Women need to think about how their life timetable intersects with their career, especially if they plan to have children. The results of this study showed that, initially, women make decisions about their careers based on the consideration of their family's timeline. Today women executives must make choices that match with their current situation as well as their future plans. However, women must also challenge the structural expectations that make these choices personal versus institutional (Eddy & Ward, 2015).

Ultimately, all these recommendations call for introspection and outward action. Women need to cultivate a network of people they can trust, both on their own campus as well as at other institutions.

Recommendations for Institutional Leaders. Based on this study, it is evident that a good leader is one who is a coach, a team player, a motivator, and committed to the job and to the entire college. Current and future executives must communicate that leading is not about power and making unilateral decisions; rather, it is about inclusion, collaboration, and teamwork, which means, at times, not relying solely on positional authority. To communicate in a team means being mindful of people in the group, using verbal and nonverbal messages to generate meanings and establish relationships, and communicating systematically. A communicative team is one that is "a collection of interacting, interdependent elements working together to form a complex whole that adapts to a changing environment" (Engleberg & Wynn, 2013, p. 5). This study showed that leaders need to be able to make tough decisions, but the best leaders regularly communicate extremely effectively and are not wary of collaboration.

Community college leaders must be able to deal effectively with and manage change through strong communication. Unlike being a faculty member, an administrative position involves constant change that occurs on a regular basis, meaning balancing many moving parts daily. Institutional leaders need to begin developing the talent required to assume top-level leadership positions. A central skill is to manage uncertainty and to be able to effectively communicate the need for change to all stakeholders. Eliminating gendered differentials is key to opening up leadership ranks to *all* potential talent.

It is important to implement leadership training collegewide on campuses. Nowadays, leadership training can be seen as generic professional development or an obligatory act based on outside demands. These trainings should focus on communication theory if we truly want to see an increase of women in leadership positions and continue to see barriers broken down. We need current leaders to address how community college can change to be more inclusive in the leadership ranks.

Recommendations for Future Research.   Several areas of future research emerged because of the current study. The following areas were identified.

1. How do male leaders communicate? Knowing how men communicate in their leadership roles, and whether these patterns are changing from historic norms, remains important. Because male leaders often do not consider their own leadership in terms of gender, it is important to know how they perceive their communication affecting others.

2. How does pay equity influence the hiring process? This study showed that pay inequities remain for women. A documentation analysis of different boards of trustees protocols on compensation can help uncover how these inequities are institutionalized. A comprehensive analysis of compensation can contribute to needed and equitable reform in educational policy and practice.

3. What is the impact of work–life decisions for women aspiring to leadership positions? Previous studies have highlighted that family affects careers (Mason, Wolfinger, & Goulden, 2013). Indeed, the women in this study discussed how they made career advancement decisions based on their family obligations. What remains unknown is whether heterosexual and homosexual women experience family dynamics in the same way. It is necessary to conduct more research on how the demands on heterosexual women differ from those on homosexual women in relation to marriage and parenting.

4. How does mentorship influence aspirations for leadership? Given the identification of mentorship as a key factor by the women in this study, further study is required to determine the benefits of same-gender mentorship in the academic workplace. Although research already exists on women and mentorship, it is of paramount importance to update the material and study the impact of mentorship as it directly affects the communication behaviors of women leaders in community colleges. When women mentor other women, the ability to engage in dual perspectives increases and discussions may become more thoughtful and purposeful.

Ultimately, these recommendations all ask researchers to study the role of communication and rhetoric to better understand how communication functions in the community college sector.

Conclusions

Throughout the interviews conducted for this study, the women spoke about how communication is of utmost importance to their leadership. It is not surprising that effective communication remains a vital contributor to the success for women leaders and that effective communication contributes to their increased use of collaboration. Communication and collaboration are essential elements that women in leadership positions use while at the same time consistently working to combat and negate stereotypes and negative perceptions of women in the academic workplace.

This study found that women leaders consider themselves successful leaders when they are focused on building relationships and creating strong teams of people who are all focused on working toward a common goal. This research also revealed that gender affects women in leadership positions because of norms and stereotypes prescribed for women, albeit not to the extent that it has in the past. Yes, women do still deal with disparate treatment, exclusion, and physical appearance, but the women in this study perceive this now occurs on a smaller scale. However, issues like pay inequity, family responsibilities, and hiring processes still remain complications that women leaders are forced to deal with on a regular basis.

In conclusion, this study highlights the role of communication for women community college leaders. Women leaders must understand the subjective nature of perception and begin to look at their team, their work, and their own behaviors with an awareness of their standpoint as women. Women need to be self-aware and continue to reflect on their experiences as women in an attempt to understand the role gender plays in their communication patterns and on their leadership and practices. In the end, the women in this study gave voice to the role of gendered communication in higher education leadership and offered recommendations on how to level the playing field to be more inclusive of women leaders.

References

Allen, B. J. (2011). *Difference matters: Communicating social identity* (2nd ed.). Long Grove, IL: Waveland Press.

American Council on Education. (2012). *The American college president: 2012.* Washington, DC: Author.

Carbaugh, D. D. (1996). *Situating selves: The communication of social identities in American scenes.* Albany, NY: State University of New York Press.

Eddy, P. L., & Ward, K. (2015). *Lean In* or opt out? Career pathways of academic women. *Change Magazine, 47*(2), 16–22.

Engleberg, I., & Wynn, D. (2013). *Working in groups: Communication principles and strategies.* Hoboken, NJ: Pearson Education.

Foss, K. A., Foss, S. K., & Griffin, C. L. (1999). *Feminist rhetorical theories.* Long Grove, IL: Waveland Press.

Lapovsky, L. (2014). *Why so few women college presidents?* Retrieved from http://www.forbes.com/sites/lucielapovsky/2014/04/13/why-so-few-women-college-presidents/

Lorber, J. (2014). Night to his day: The social construction of gender. In R. Groner & J. F. O'Hara (Eds.), *Composing gender: A Bedford spotlight reader* (pp. 54–65). Boston, MA: Bedford/St. Martin's.

Mason, M. A., Wolfinger, N. H., & Goulden, M. (2013). *Do babies matter?: Gender and family in the ivory tower.* New Brunswick, NJ: Rutgers University Press.

Rakow, L. F., & Wackwitz, L. A. (Eds.). (2004). *Feminist communication theory: Selections in context.* Thousand Oaks, CA: Sage.

Rossman, G. B., & Rallis, S.F. (2012). *Learning in the field: An introduction to qualitative research.* Thousand Oaks, CA: Sage.

West, C., & Zimmerman, D. H. (1987). Doing gender. *Gender and Society, 1*(2), 125–151.

White, J. (2013). *HERS at forty: Shaping a new vision of women's (and men's) liberation.* Retrieved from http://archive.aacu.org/ocww/volume41_2/feature.cfm?section=2

AMY FARA EDWARDS, EdD, is a tenured communication studies professor at Oxnard College in southern California and is also the chair for the Visual and Performing Arts department and an Academic Senate executive.

NEW DIRECTIONS FOR COMMUNITY COLLEGES • DOI: 10.1002/cc

3

This chapter reports on interviews with women leaders finding that transformational learning contributes to new mental models for leadership.

Changing Leadership: Taking a Stand by "Moving the Needle" for Women's Leadership in Community Colleges

Rosemary Gillett-Karam

> If one asked me to what do I think one must principally attribute the singular prosperity and growing force of [America], I would answer that it is the superiority of its women.
>
> (de Tocqueville, 1835/2000, p. 576)

Almost 200 years after de Tocqueville's observations, the theme of his acknowledgement remains pertinent; reporting on research findings highlights how capitalizing on women's abilities as leaders can allow prosperity to grow in American community colleges. The effort to expand the number of women in leadership roles is now being explored as a matter of urgency by the American Council of Education (ACE) in a national effort titled Moving the Needle (MtN). Explaining "where we are now, where we want to be, and why now" the following data are revealed by ACE (2016):

- Women occupy 26% of all college presidencies.
- Women are outnumbered by men on all governing boards by two to one.
- Women of color earn 54% of men's earnings.
- Women earn 59% of all academic degrees.
- Women comprise 48% of professors (although men as full professors greatly outnumber women).
- Women represent over 60% of students in colleges.
- Sixty percent of all current college presidents are over age 61. (p. 1)

NEW DIRECTIONS FOR COMMUNITY COLLEGES, no. 179, Fall 2017 © 2017 Wiley Periodicals, Inc.
Published online in Wiley Online Library (wileyonlinelibrary.com) • DOI: 10.1002/cc.20260

The goal of the MtN effort is to capture the attention of academia and create urgency to increase the numbers of women as leaders in higher education and to "burst" the pipeline myth, which purports there are too few women qualified for leadership positions (ACE, 2016). The mission of the MtN is to advance demographically diverse women to senior-level decision-making and policymaking leadership positions.

This chapter focuses on how community college presidents, midlevel administrators and faculty, and members of boards of trustees are responding to ACE's call to advance the changing and growing roles of women as leaders. More than 30 respondents, including current, retired, interim, new, and seasoned presidents and culturally diverse women presidents participated in this study and offered their views, as did active board of trustees members, and college midlevel administrators and faculty (some of whom had been ACE Fellows). In the array of American community college female presidents is a diverse group of women from tribal colleges, historically black community colleges, Hispanic-serving colleges, and from the designation of minority-serving colleges (MSI). Following is a historical review of the leadership literature, including a review of four 10-year phases of research and literature specifically about women in leadership roles in community colleges. Next, findings from the study regarding observations and perceptions of women's continuing goals for leadership are presented and interpreted. Finally, suggestions are posited for continuing studies of the evolving role of women as community college leaders.

Previous Research and Phases of Study

Nearly a quarter of a century ago, I wrote about how women were underrepresented in community college leadership (Gillett-Karam, 1988). At the time, only 8% of community college presidents were women. Since then growth has been slow, only about a 1%–1.5% increase in women presidents every 2 years. For women of color the percentage of community college presidencies rose initially but then began to decline in the last several years (American Association of Community Colleges [AACC], 2015). Beginning around 1980, a discourse community (Nystrand, 1982), which included researchers writing about women as leaders of community colleges, studied women's development differently.

Four Phases of Literature Development.   Gilligan's (1982) work initiated the first phase of focused works on women's development and successes. Women scholars (Gillett-Karam, 1988; Moore, 1988; Mulder, 1983; Twombly, 1988) wrote about women as leaders in community colleges. Twombly (1988) advocated a view of women's leadership as a distinctively women-centered form of leadership. This period marked the *introductory advocacy phase* of literature focusing on women's roles as community college leaders; most of these writers wrote about seated women presidents and their frameworks reported on skills or attributes of leaders, usually from a behavioral perspective.

By the 1990s, a second phase of research on women leaders emerged. This second phase, *narrowing the influence* of women as leaders in community colleges, focused on pathways, differences and similarities between male and female leaders, and revealing differences in cultures of leaders (Amey, 1999). Here, issues such as place boundedness, family responsibilities, and diversity were explored (Sagaria & Rychener, 2004; Vaughan, 2001). In this phase, a focus on the role of networking, mentoring, leadership development programs, and the evolution of leadership characteristics and skills relating to both women and men occurred.

The third phase of research about women began at the turn of the 21st century. This phase focused on the *need for change in identifying new leadership*. Early 21st century writers remained true to the psychological focus of leadership that looks at human behavior. Stout-Stewart (2005) examined leadership patterns and behaviors and included discussion on race, educational level, discrimination, and leadership gaps. Amey and VanDerLinden (2002) also pursued their research on career paths and reported how pathways were changing, although internal hires and careers building from within the community college displayed an internal labor market.

By 2010, a fourth phase of research emerged as writers began to *refocus the context* of leadership. Many articles appeared focusing on calls for more women leaders for institutions of higher learning; other articles and books reintroduced a changing image of leadership in the community college (Eddy, 2008, 2010; Nevarez & Wood, 2010). Eddy (2010) argued that the social construction of gender, gendered organizations, and gendered communication as constructs would continue "separating" men and women as future leaders. Townsend and Twombly (2007) reopened inquiry about the climate for diversity and women in community colleges, which set the stage for current research.

Looking Forward.   The current phase of research recognizes the need to replace talk with action. Demands for more equality among leaders and in representativeness are increasing. Current research focuses on learning as a leadership skill (Amey, 2013) given the aging of leaders and the corresponding prediction of large numbers of retirees (Vaughan & Weiss, 2006). New construction of multidimensional leadership models (Eddy, 2010) sets the stage for progress for women community college leaders. Joining in with support for developing women as leaders to achieve parity and equal representation are several national associations (e.g., the American Association of Community Colleges, the American Council of Education, Higher Education Resource Services [HERS]).

The focus on new models of leadership pays particular attention to race as well as gender (Bower, 2010; Britton, 2013; Turner, 2007). More research on the intersection of race and gender needs to occur regarding ways to "move the needle" for women of color as holdover views of women leaders from the 1980s persist (ACE, 2016). Yet, stagnation and impediments of movement for women, and especially women of color, as leaders among community colleges remain evident.

Study Background

This study focused on diverse representation of women community college leaders. To achieve a range of representation of voices, I sought to include not only presidents but also other midlevel administrators and board members to provide a balanced picture of contemporary community college leadership. A panel of academic colleagues was responsible for suggesting names for the study, and I ultimately interviewed a total of 30 participants. I used transformative learning as a theoretical framework to highlight leaders' policies and actions (Habermas, 1981; Mezirow, 2000).

Building on the MtN initiative, I sought to investigate how Mezirow's (2000) transformative learning theory influenced the experiences of the women in this study. A learning orientation helps in the development of leadership (Amey, 2013; Habermas, 1981), resulting in new knowledge created through the transformative experiences (Mezirow, 2000). Central to Mezirow's conceptualization of transformative learning theory is disruption and dissonance that trigger unlearning and relearning, ultimately leading to a transformation in how one understands situations and in this case leading to significant change.

Findings

This study identified three main findings. First, transformative learning for the women presented challenges in how they reconciled their leadership in the current context of leadership expectations. The participants noted the ways in which the confines of current definitions of leadership roles prevented them from being authentic. Second, how women constructed their advocacy for change influenced how they perceived their effectiveness as leaders. Finally, the position of the women leaders created particular challenges.

Transformative Learning as Challenge.   Women as leaders in organizations "produced a better bottom line, return on investment, and return on equity; they improved corporate oversight, increased productivity, and enhanced employee engagement" (ACE, 2016, p. 2). With fewer women than men in key leadership roles in community colleges, it is important to understand more about how learning contributes to leadership (Amey, 2013).

Most of the women presidents in this study had impressive biographies, but I focus on one president in particular who fought to restructure the institutional designation of her college after taking office in 2007. Her transformative learning and disruption of sameness of understanding in traditional modes led her to convince others, through advocacy, to share her rethinking of the mission of her institution. The college, founded in the late 1800s, had a new emphasis centered on a greater democratic mission and vision of the campus. The president reconfigured her institution to focus on its minority student majority. She leads by articulating and convincing others to relearn and reflect on the changing identity of community colleges and their students and by turning thought into action.

Another award-winning president noted how she never personally reveals her accomplishments. She highlighted her focus on tangible community inclusion and relationships, adding, "My recognition is second to the institution's growth and changing identity." Recently, her college received funding from the city to construct a new building on her campus for a new program, and she has received several million dollars from a new community source. She attributed her success to "sensemaking from the community stakeholders and friend making of key movers and shakers; I had to first get it straight in my head." How the president engaged in transformational learning allowed her to make sense of the new initiatives and to gain buy-in from partners.

One of the longest tenured female community college presidents in this study began her college presidency in the early 1980s. She recognized, and "pushed" her staff to learn about the intricacies of leadership in a changing world. She not only succeeded in leading her own campus to change, but she can count numerous "wins" among former administrators and staff who have become community college leaders. "Waiting was never my strong suit," she explained, "as leaders we have to make things happen then reconstruct reality." This long-serving president's success over time grew from her commitment to ongoing learning for herself and her understanding of the importance of meaning making for others.

A new college president introduced a framework for leadership training based in part on her own learning. Viewing leadership as a "calling to serve," she modeled herself as a trainer for new leaders. Her "calling," she explained, was to hire the most innovative leadership advocates to come to her campus. She used role-play to help participants evaluate campus strategies and to understand how various roles helped support innovations. Participants also produced an essay explaining the process and outcomes of their design. This leader questioned assumptions and modeled the idea of continuous learning with others as she sought to develop for leading on campus.

Another participant was a system chancellor. This leader discussed her attention to growing numbers of veterans, to incoming ethnic minorities, and to large numbers of prisoners, those she identified as "all ignored and voiceless" in her community. This focus on other is an integral part of her college's and her community's identity (deBeauvoir, 1949). She added,

My staff and I originally had pushbacks from funders who rejected our ideas, but as we pursued our new vision and conditions for change, and persevered and persevered, ultimately we were granted large endowments—the payoff was that each of these newly identified groups were succeeding, thus the colleges and their communities were also succeeding.

Her analytics of accomplishments of these three groups continue to astound community stakeholders whom she says ask her all the time, "What's next on your agenda?"

Another president used the metaphor of the blind men in a room with an elephant in which each identified different parts of the elephant differently; they did not envision the whole animal. She explained, "Perhaps, as I believe, the 'right' people were not in the room." She discussed her approach to developmental education in which a cohort of faculty studied the developmental education students on her campuses for a few years and embarked on a series of interventions they labeled learning disruptions. Their program, although not immediately popular, has become a national success, with analytics to prove their unlearning and relearning as a group of committed administrators and faculty have made a positive difference in the lives of their students. This same college president is a strong supporter of women's leadership. "Diversity and inclusion must direct our new thinking," she has advocated as she has led her own college and the associations she has served to offer advancement to diverse women.

Not all the participants in this study evidenced transformative learning. Pointedly, two presidents interviewed expressed disappointment as the legacy of their careers by reflecting on the "downward spiral" of both their institutions and themselves. Both presidents saw decreasing enrollments, financial exigency, accreditation ills, and an aging, disagreeable faculty as issues so insurmountable they could not overcome them. Both presidents blamed their situations as "out of their control" and commented on the "misuse of power and interfering control by trustees." This lack of agency resulted in these leaders not examining their underlying beliefs and assumptions to make sense of and ameliorate their situations. They admitted to being "overpowered" in their positions, which ultimately led to their early retirements.

The Role of Advocacy in Leading.   The women presidents in this study proved themselves unique in their leadership and in their advocacy of community college education. One president, who held a position in her state's governing body, began the job by first traveling throughout the state and holding more than 50 small meetings with constituencies. A key outcome of these meetings was a desire by stakeholders for the community college to build up workforce capacities, but at the time, the "popularity" of this mission focus was severely diminished in community college's programs. To accomplish this work, she focused on restructuring collaborations between the college and business. Aligned with this advocacy for the college was a concurrent advocacy for women in traditionally male-dominated work positions.

Advocacy for minorities was also relevant to presidents who represent Hispanic, Asian, and African American cultures. For example, a Latina college president advocates for a new pipeline of leadership; she commented that qualified Latinas needed "experiences to learn a way to get into the pipeline." To support her advocacy, she developed a leadership fellows program as part of the National Community College Hispanic Council (NC-CHC). Both the NCCHC and the National Council on Black American Affairs (NCBAA) have training programs to promote minority leadership development. These councils offer both mentoring and networking opportunities and in each instance, a substantial number of their participants have become college presidents. What pushed this president in her advocacy was learning that among the over 100 colleges in her state only five Latinas were trustees of community colleges. Further, she had also discovered that 80% of Latinos students in her state start their college experiences at a community college (22% is the national number reported by AACC, 2016) and that community college faculty were least represented by this ethnic group (4%; Snyder & Dillow, 2013). This leader sought specific strategies that could help Hispanics achieve representativeness in leadership roles in community colleges and has involved others in this effort.

Native Americans represent another minority serving in community college leadership positions. Only 2% of community college presidents are Native Americans and these leaders usually lead tribal colleges. Presidents of tribal colleges are adamant in their promises to retain and disseminate the language, practices, and culture of American Indians. One female president summed up these beliefs saying, "We cannot forget we are the original Americans, and as such, our traditions and culture form the basis of the American culture—we bring this reality to our students and communities." The intersection of gender and ethnicity provided a source of joint advocacy for minority women leaders in this study.

Like Latina and Native American women presidents, Asians have little representation in the top-leadership role on campus (Asian presidents make up less than 1.5% of all college presidents; ACE, 2012). Yet, these scant numbers are not due to a problem with the pipeline. I found several examples of leaders who challenge this myth. One Asian participant explained the social position of minorities in community colleges "like the Hertz logo—we're number two." That position, she says, "makes us try harder and allows us to take risks." Reflecting her risk-taking, she hired a critical mass of women and people of color in faculty and senior administrative positions, positions lacking this representation.

Advocacy in leading aligned with the values for the women in this study. The women of color in particular highlighted how they used the leverage of their position to help advocate for social justice and how this advocacy aligned well with the mission of the community college as a point of access.

Position Challenges for Midlevel Leaders and Board Members. Women and leaders of color are in short supply in high-level administration positions in community colleges. A key challenge for administrators and staff in community colleges was their place boundedness. Despite aspirations for leadership positions, being "tied" as a subordinate or place-bound position in their institution did not offer them a pathway up the career ladder. Yet, these women acquired leadership skills and reported accomplishments tied to issue resolution, such as working on reaccreditation, attending meetings in which they were placeholders for their superiors, and taking on issues from the press. These early coping strategies proved important when the women reached top-level positions. Still, midlevel women administrators expressed more about professional barriers than benefits, which raises the urgency of advancing administrative positions that feed to the presidency.

Boards of trustees are the hiring body for the college and serve as linchpins for changing the portrait of community college presidencies. However, as 80% of all community college trustees are White (Association of Community College Trustees [ACCT], 2014), the issue of diversity remains a problem. I queried female board members of community colleges about their role in choosing presidents. One board member from the south had been on her board for over 40 years and explained she "just knew the time had come to hire an African American president," even though she had to lead the effort among her fellow board members to do so. "Best choice I ever made," she added, "as our president has made a world of difference to our institution, our community, and our staffs and students." The role of women on boards of trustees can help open up the pipeline for hiring more diverse presidents.

Another board member, herself an ethnic minority among few similar representatives, was somewhat confounded by her position as a trustee.

> When I got here, I had to fight tooth and nail to convince fellow trustees to trust my views and to reformulate ancient policies that were not attuned to a changing identity of students. While our students are majority African American, our administration and faculty are not, clearly a concern of our students.

Did she prevail? "Slowly," she said. "Our most critical problem was board interference in the management of the college, we had a large turnover of presidents in a short period of time, and the board began to think they were the stable link of day-to-day management." Ultimately, their state legislature had to issue a law disallowing their interference in the daily management of the college.

Upper level administrators and boards of trustees hold sway on campus and make decisions that have long-lasting consequences. How presidents are hired, who gets leadership development opportunities, and how effective presidents learn how to lead are central issues to resolve to increase the diversity of community college leaders.

Recommendations

Emerging from this study are several recommendations for practice. Attention to these strategies can help increase the number of women leading in community colleges and expand the diversity of college presidents.

1. Women of color have had limited success in rising to leadership positions in community colleges. Initiatives like the ACE *Moving the Needle* can help change these data, but only if university training programs continue to highlight the benefits of women as leaders, and if mentors (both male and female) become more vocal and dedicated to the urgency of this movement. Programs such as the NCBAA, Presidents' Roundtable, and the National Community College Council (NCCC) can continue developing potential leaders. In the past several years, over 500 leaders have emerged from such programs.
2. Parity remains an objective for all women to rise as leaders of community colleges, not only as presidents. It is important to focus on midlevel leadership (Eddy, Garza Mitchell, & Amey, 2016) as these positions serve not only as points for succession training for upper level leaders but also as a means to exert leadership in their own right. Parity is also required on boards of trustees, and here the ACCT can take a leadership role to increase national representation of women and leaders of color.
3. University graduate programs in leadership should continue to recruit promising administrators and staff from community colleges, as the doctoral degree is a sought-after credential when recruiting new presidents. As well, these doctoral programs can help place students in intern positions in nearby community colleges to help promote working in the 2-year sector as a career goal. Online training programs can also be beneficial as long as work is relatable to real-life practitioner experiences for students. Course work targeting community college faculty is also critical, especially for faculty of color, as faculty serve on the frontlines in their work with students. Community colleges also have a role to play in identifying and supporting their "best and brightest" for leadership development.
4. Current leaders and trustees must take a stand to demand equal representation of women and leaders of color in positions of leadership in America's community colleges. Pointing to the pipeline as the reason for the lack of parity in leadership positions is a myth now long

debunked. Instead, a new narrative must be created that demands the development of *all* talent within the community college to achieve equity in leadership positions.

References

American Association of Community Colleges. (2015). *Fact sheet*. Washington, DC: Author.

American Association of Community Colleges. (2016). *Fact sheet*. Washington, DC: Author.

American Council on Education. (2012). *The American college president: 2012*. Washington, DC: Author.

American Council on Education. (2016). *Moving the needle: Advancing women in higher education leadership*. Washington, DC: Author. Retrieved from http://www.acenet.edu/news-room/Documents/Moving-the-Needle-Trifold-Brochure.pdf

Amey, M. J. (1999). Navigating the raging river: Reconciling issues of identity, inclusion and administrative practice. In K. M. Shaw, J. R. Valadez, & R. A. Rhoads (Eds.), *Community colleges as cultural texts: Qualitative explorations of organizational and student cultures* (pp. 59–82). Albany, NY: SUNY Press.

Amey, M. J. (2013). Leadership: Community college transitions. In J. S. Levin & S. T. Kater (Eds.), *Understanding community colleges* (pp. 135–152). New York, NY: Routledge.

Amey, M. J., & VanDerLinden, K. (2002). *Career paths for community college leaders*. Washington, DC: American Association of Community Colleges.

Association of Community College Trustees. (2014). *The leadership imperative*. Washington, DC: Author.

Bower, B. (2010). *Answering the call: African American women in higher education leadership*. Sterling, VA: Stylus.

Britton, M. C. (2013). Race/ethnicity, attitudes and living with parents. *Journal of Marriage and Family, 75*(4), 995–1013.

deBeauvoir, S. (1949). *The second sex*. New York, NY: Random House/Knopf.

de Tocqueville, A. (1835/2000). *Democracy in America* (H. C. Mansfield, Trans.). Chicago, IL: University of Chicago Press.

Eddy, P. L. (2008). Reflections of women leading community colleges. *Community College Enterprise, 14*(1), 49–66.

Eddy, P. L. (2010). *Community college leadership: A multidimensional model for leading change*. Sterling, VA: Stylus.

Eddy, P. L., Garza Mitchell, R., & Amey, M. J. (2016, December 2). Leading from the middle. *Chronicle of Higher Education, 68*(15), A48.

Gillett-Karam, R. (1988). *Transformational leadership and community college presidents: Are there gender differences?* (Doctoral dissertation). University of Texas at Austin.

Gilligan, C. (1982). *In a different voice*. Cambridge, MA: Harvard University.

Habermas, J. (1981). *Theory of communicative action*. Boston, MA: Beacon Press.

Mezirow, J. (2000). *Learning as transformation: Critical perspectives on a theory in progress*. San Francisco, CA: Jossey-Bass.

Moore, K. M. (1988). Administrative careers: Multiple pathways to leadership positions. In M. F. Green (Ed.), *Leaders for a new era: Strategies for higher education* (pp. 159–180). New York, NY: American Council on Education and Macmillan.

Mulder, A. E. (1983). *Women in educational administration: Paths and profiles* (Doctoral dissertation). University of Michigan, Ann Arbor.

Nevarez, C., & Wood, J. L. (2010). *Community college leadership and administration*. New York, NY: Peter Lang.

Nystrand, M. (1982). *What writers know*. New York, NY: Academic.

Sagaria, M. A. D., & Rychener, M. A. (2004). Inside leadership circles and the managerial quagmire: Key influences on women administrators' mobility and opportunity in US higher education. *The politics of gender and education* (pp. 103–116). London, UK: Palgrave Macmillan.

Snyder, T. D., & Dillow, S. A. (2013). *Digest of education statistics 2013*. Washington, DC: U.S. Department of Education, National Center for Education Statistics.

Stout-Stewart, S. (2005). Female community college presidents: Effective leadership patterns and behaviors. *Community College Journal of Research and Practice*, 29(4), 303–315.

Townsend, B. J., & Twombly, S. (2007). Community college faculty, overlooked and undervalued. [*ASHE Higher Education Report*, 32(6), 1–163]. San Francisco, CA: Jossey-Bass.

Turner, C. S. (2007). Pathways to presidency: Biographical sketches of women of color. *Harvard Educational Review*, 77(1), 1–38.

Twombly, S. (1988). Administrative labor markets. *Journal of Higher Education*, 59(6), 668–689.

Vaughan, G. B. (2001). *The community college presidency: 2001*. Washington, DC: American Association of Community Colleges.

Vaughan, G. B., & Weiss, I. (2006). *The community college presidency: 2006*. Washington, DC: American Association of Community Colleges.

ROSEMARY GILLETT-KARAM *is an associate professor of higher education in the Department of Advanced Studies, Leadership, and Policy at Morgan State College and serves as the director of the Community College Leadership Doctoral Program.*

4

This chapter draws on a longitudinal study about women faculty, work–family, and career advancement in community colleges. The study found that the participants, though highly satisfied with their careers and qualified for administration, are largely uninterested in moving to more senior administrative positions.

"Good" Places to Work: Women Faculty, Community Colleges, Academic Work, and Family Integration

Kelly Ward, Lisa Wolf-Wendel

Research about faculty has increasingly focused on different aspects of family life and how it shapes an academic career. For example, Mason, Wolfinger, and Goulden (2013) have adopted longitudinal perspectives to see how family and career formation intersect. They found that "babies do matter" and that having a child for early career faculty affects long-term career and family outcomes (p. 1). Other work–family research looks at fathers (Sallee, 2013) and college policy (Lester & Sallee, 2009), and our own research looks at different aspects of academic motherhood (Ward & Wolf-Wendel, 2012). A conclusion to be drawn from the collective research about work and family in the academy is that experiences are largely shaped by institutional setting—where a person works shapes the interface of work and family.

In the larger academic motherhood project that informs this chapter (Ward & Wolf-Wendel, 2012), we found that faculty in community colleges talk about work and family in markedly different ways than do women in comprehensive/regional institutions, liberal arts colleges, or research universities. In particular, we found that community college women faculty members identify their institutions as "good" places to work for a woman who wants to have an academic career and a family (Wolf-Wendel, Ward, & Twombly, 2007). In short, we found that community colleges are perceived as a good academic career choice for women wanting to have a career and a family—a finding that holds steady for women at early and midcareer stages (Ward & Wolf-Wendel, 2012).

NEW DIRECTIONS FOR COMMUNITY COLLEGES, no. 179, Fall 2017 © 2017 Wiley Periodicals, Inc.
Published online in Wiley Online Library (wileyonlinelibrary.com) • DOI: 10.1002/cc.20261

There are several factors present in the community college setting that contribute to why they are good places to work. First, the scant majority of full-time faculty members at community college are women, including a majority in part-time positions (Chronicle of Higher Education, 2015) and the number of women administrators is also greater than in any other sector (American Council on Education, 2012). Community colleges, in terms of numbers, have become a feminized space within higher education. Second, teaching is the main focus of community colleges (an aspect of faculty life with which women are associated); research and publications are not a focus of employment—an aspect of faculty life that has been a greater concern for women than men (Leslie, 2006; Mason et al., 2013; Perna, 2001). The purpose of this chapter is to more fully explore how the community college context is a "good choice" as a place to work for women. In particular, we focus on women faculty members at midcareer stages so we can examine their progression in the academic career pipeline.

In line with the overall purpose of this volume about constructions of gender in community colleges, the focus of the chapter is situated in ongoing research that looks at different aspects of gender and community colleges (e.g., Drake, 2008). As evident throughout this volume, topics related to gender in community colleges are of interest given the relative success of the numbers of women who study, work, and lead in community colleges (especially relative to other sectors of higher education). The topic is also important given current concerns about career trajectories at community colleges—in particular, career succession and the preparation of faculty for leadership roles in community colleges (Garza Mitchell & Eddy, 2008; Lester, 2008; Mackey, 2008). Although women have made greater strides in terms of representation throughout all stages of the pipeline from student to president in community colleges, they still remain underrepresented in the senior ranks of administration. The goal here is to look more closely at midcareer faculty to explore how gender, academic work, and family shape the ascent to leadership.

Perspectives From the Literature

Recognizing the conflicts that can take place between biological clocks and tenure clocks, research about work and family for faculty has increased through the past 10 years. This attention reflects changes in the academic labor market, the influx of women into higher education at multiple levels, the demands of millennial faculty, and a recognition by institutions of higher education that work/faculty considerations are an important factor in faculty recruitment and retention (Trower, 2010). A majority of this research is focused on tenure-track faculty who have children and who work at 4-year institutions (e.g., Mason et al., 2013; Perna, 2001). There has been very limited research about community college faculty and work–life issues (e.g., Wolf-Wendel et al., 2007). Some research suggests that women doctoral degree holders seeking faculty positions may opt to work at community colleges because they feel that these institutions are more supportive to balancing work and family than are tenure-track positions at 4-year institutions (Perna, 2001; Ward & Wolf-Wendel, 2012). It is important to study the extent to which these beliefs are justified and how these beliefs influence the career trajectory of academic mothers in community colleges.

Despite the achievements of women faculty in community colleges, it is still important to study how gender and parental status play a role in the career trajectory of these women (Lester, 2008; Twombly & Townsend, 2008). Full-time faculty members at community colleges take on expanded roles given the prevalence of part-time faculty who tend to focus on teaching and have limited time on campus (Kezar & Sam, 2010). It is important to examine how full-time women faculty members manage their multiple roles as faculty given their simultaneous roles as mothers. In seeking gender equity in leadership positions, it is important to understand how work–life integration factors into faculty perspectives about pursuing administrative positions. Previous research and commentary indicate that women often avoid senior leadership positions given tension between work and family expectations and roles (Drake, 2008; Garza Mitchell & Eddy, 2008; Sandberg, 2013). The findings from this study will contribute to fuller understanding of community colleges as good places to work.

Conceptual Perspectives: Feminism and Choice

Women continue to make the greatest strides and have the greatest representation in institutions that are perceived as less prestigious (e.g., community colleges), in positions that are marginalized in traditional academic terms (i.e., nontenure track and part-time positions) and in disciplines that tend to be marginalized in terms of knowledge production and institutional value systems (e.g., education, humanities; Allan, 2011). One way to look at the progress and position of women in higher education is from the lens of choice. That is, women choose to work part time or in nontenure-track positions, they choose to work in community colleges or other institutions perceived as less prestigious, they choose particular disciplines, and above all, they choose to have children. Collectively these choices contribute to the current representation of women faculty at community colleges. The focus on individual choice is also a way to examine the community college context for academic mothers as good places to work. To be certain, choice is a banner concept for women, feminism, and the women's movement. What gets lost, however, in explaining the status of women in higher education as a matter of individual choice is how these choices are influenced by power and gender norms in institutions (Baca-Zinn, 2000; Gill, 2007). Using perspectives that emerge from feminist theory provides a tool to critically analyze the choices women make and how these choices influence career outcomes.

New Directions for Community Colleges • DOI: 10.1002/cc

Feminist theory helps to frame the lives of women in a larger societal context in which gender and power shape how people interface with the workplace and the roles they play in their families (Allan, 2011; Ferguson, 1997; Thayer-Bacon, Stone, & Sprecher, 2013). Allan's (2011, p. 18) work helped us conceptualize key components of all types of feminism:

- Sex and gender inequality exists and is central to social relations and the structure of social institutions.
- Sex and gender inequality is not "natural" or essential but a product of social relations.
- Sex and gender inequality should be eliminated through social change.

As a means to further grapple with choice as it relates to work and family decisions for academic mothers, we use liberal and poststructural views of feminism. Liberal feminism posits that women have the same natural rights as men (Donovan, 2012) and argues for equal opportunity in the workforce (Acker, 1987). The notion that men and women are equal and that policies and practices ought to level the playing field for men and women to compete on an equal footing are foundational to a liberal feminist view (Donovan, 2012). Yet, existing research (e.g., Sallee, 2013) shows that adding more women or creating more policies clearly is not enough to level the playing field for women at work. Liberal views provide a starting point but come up short to fully explain gender and power in the academic milieu.

In contrast, a poststructural view of feminism links gender to power structures (Allan, Iverson, & Ropers-Huilman, 2009). The poststructural lens is helpful to examine constraints women still face as they seek to accomplish the dual roles of mother and faculty member in the academic environment by looking at the interplay of structure and discourse. Focusing only on policies and programs as means to create equity, without looking at underlying culture and structure, is essentially dealing with the symptom and not the real cause of inequity.

A poststructuralist view helps to uncover deeply held assumptions about the workplace and particularly how gender shapes those assumptions (Allan, 2011). Feminist analysis is particularly important when looking at community college settings because at least superficially it appears that these institutions are "good" places to work for women. What remains unknown, however, is how women community college faculty members make choices about their careers and how workplace and societal norms influence those choices.

Research Background

For the past 15 years, we have been engaged in a longitudinal study to see how women manage work and family in the context of the academic career.

The first phase of the study looked at women ($n = 120$) in full-time faculty positions at research universities, comprehensive colleges, liberal arts colleges, and community colleges when they were early career (i.e., first 5 years of their positions) and when they had young children (i.e., under age 5) to see how they managed work and family early in their careers. The sample included 30 faculty from each institutional type. The first phase of this project was conducted in 2000. The second phase of the study looked at faculty ($n = 88$) who were early midcareer (i.e., in years 7–12 of their career) to see how their careers evolved and to examine their leadership aspirations. The second phase was conducted in 2007. Community college women faculty members have been central to the study in phases one ($n = 30$) and two ($n = 27$). Details about the methodology and full findings of the study are available in *Academic Motherhood: How Faculty Manage Work and Family* (Ward & Wolf-Wendel, 2012). The third phase of the study, conducted in 2016, includes 17 of the original group of community college women faculty to see how work and family has evolved for them in the "mid" midcareer phase, and examined leadership intentions, aspirations, and experiences. This chapter focuses on findings about work, family, and career development for the community college participants across the three phases of the study.

Findings

The findings from all phases of the project point to community colleges as deliberate and good choices for women wanting to have families and academic careers. The choice to work in community colleges is related to the mission of teaching and the ability to work with students, and a deemphasis on traditional research. An additional element to choosing the community college setting was based on location and place. The participants in the study, in part, chose community colleges to pursue their careers based on geographical constraints in addition to a commitment to teaching.

The Community College Choice.   For many of the community college women in this study, the choice and conscious decision to work in a community college stemmed from reactions to prior work experiences and their own graduate school experiences that were perceived to be less flexible for family life or less enjoyable than teaching at the community college. The majority of the women in the study had experience working in other settings before teaching at the community college, a finding distinct to the community college faculty in the sample. The comparative lens made them see the community college as a good choice relative to previous positions. For example, one participant in the study shared, "I have no doubt that this is what I want to do because each morning that I woke up to go to my clinic job, I didn't want to go. I dreaded it. I hated life." Another compared her faculty job to her former work in government and banking and said, "I think it [working at a community college] is more grounded and real. Everything is a crisis from my experience in corporate America." The women faculty understood how their current choice of work was better than previous employment.

Many of the women noted that the community college was a great place to work as a faculty member and a parent. In fact, most commented on how many other working parents there were on campus. As one woman explained, "I am in a department with a number of other women who are also mothers, so there is … an understanding among my departmental colleagues of what this life is like. I consider myself very lucky in terms of my colleagues not just in my department but also within the larger institution." Other women echoed this sentiment explaining, "I am really fortunate in that almost all of my colleagues have children." Part of what makes community colleges a "good" place to work, according to our respondents, is the perception, as summarized by a participant, that "faculty are often able to negotiate a more flexible work schedule around school drop offs or activities for their kids." Another summed up this sentiment this way: "Many of them [faculty] are working here for that exact same reason, they want to be involved with their family, and have time outside of work to be involved with their family." Being able to work in an organization in which having a family was supported was critical for the participants.

In addition to seeing the choice to work in a community college as a "good" choice compared to previous professional positions and for the ability to focus on family, participants also chose to work in community colleges based on negative views of working in a 4-year institution. Faculty in the study mentioned their choice to work in a community college to avoid the life they saw their graduate school faculty leading. A typical response came from one respondent who explained, "Most of the women … who were my [faculty] mentors did not have families or children, so that bothered me …. Is that going to be the sacrifice I make to work here [at a 4-year institution]?" Another respondent stated,

> I can only imagine what it would be like at a research university. God, no, I would never choose that for my life. It's my conception of it, and maybe my conception is wrong. The whole publish or perish, the pressure on you and that kind of thing.

Still another commented, "When I got to the community college, I thought 'this is it.' I'm not into the 4-year or university because I don't want to do all that research and that's not my cup of tea." The theme of avoiding the publish or perish trap was linked explicitly with the desire to have a family, as explained by another respondent: "It seemed that it would be very difficult for us to balance my husband's job, my job, raising children, and the whole university career track." One respondent summed up her choice this way:

A number of people that I work with, in fact, are women who have kids, and they have doctorates and could work at a number of different places. But, they chose this route just because it is a friendly environment for compromise as far as your hours go. It allows you to have a life outside of work.

To be fair, although many made the final choice about working at a community college based on the negative perceptions associated with faculty life at research universities, they were also drawn to the community college setting because of a love of teaching and a desire to serve the kinds of students who attend these institutions.

Career Development and Leadership Choices.   In the second and third phases of the study, the majority of community college women faculty (all but three from the original sample) remained in their original positions and maintained their commitment to teaching and working with students. In addition, about half of them had moved into midlevel leadership positions at the time of the second interviews (e.g., unit directors, program leaders, project directors, grants administrators, etc.). At the time of the second interview, the majority of participants mentioned the possibility of eventually moving into administration when their children were older and out of the house. In the third phase of the study, however, the findings illustrate that the press for seeking leadership positions had lessened. As one participant shared, "I don't want to go any higher than I am because I don't like . . . bureaucracy. I'm very happy where I am. Someone else can have that big paying job and I'll stay right here." Similarly, another participant talked about how her initial aspirations for senior-level administration had changed the more she took on administrative tasks. "I don't see myself going higher up. I had aspirations to be a dean and I'm not going to do that. I like where I am." For some of the women in the study, the time to move into administration would be now because their children were older and they were more established in their careers. Yet, most avoided moving into senior-level positions —instead they opted to remain in the full-time teaching ranks and were starting to think about retirement. Choosing to move into administration (or not) sheds light on a different aspect of agency and choice in that the participants are intentionally choosing not to pursue leadership.

Time and Energy Choices.   Another important element of choice that emerges from the interviews highlights how these women in midcareer decide to spend their time and energy. Many of the women noted that at this stage of their career they feel they have a fair amount of autonomy to home in on the parts of their jobs that they find most satisfying. When these women were more junior, they felt pressure to behave in certain ways or to engage in certain aspects of their job; as they have advanced in their careers, they feel freer to engage in those aspects of the job they most enjoy and find gratifying. As one of our women explained, "I do feel satisfied and I'm at a point in my career that I can say 'no.'" Another participant stated,

"It feels time for letting the days be directed more by my goals instead of what others need."

Mostly, what these women enjoy about their positions is teaching. A typical response follows: "I certainly enjoy being a mother, I enjoy teaching as well. My schedule allows me to do the things I like." Another woman, who had done some intensive service right after she got tenure noted that she was excited to go back to teaching before she retired, "to end my career with what made me the happiest at the beginning of my career, working more directly with students." Another commented, "I went back to the classroom and I'm not looking back." A major theme from the interviews was related to a passion for teaching. One woman captured this sentiment best as she explained, "The students are awesome and I love them. I'm not here to create chemists. I am here to inspire my students to become interested in the sciences." The overall findings convey an ongoing commitment to the teaching norms and the students who attend community colleges.

The desire to be both a "good" mother and "good" teacher at the same time was a clear preference for these women and they felt like the community college context facilitated that combination. As one respondent shared, "I feel good about the choices we made, we did put our kids first and we did a lot of that balancing, and I'm glad we did it." These women are vital members of their academic communities. They are also still active in family life even with children older and sometimes living on their own. A major finding from the data is that at mid-midcareer, participants choose to prioritize the things about the job that they love and to deemphasize those aspects of their positions that were less enjoyable in an effort to have overall work–life integration.

As community colleges grapple with anticipated leadership shortages and work toward greater gender equity in leadership positions, it is important to understand the role that family plays in women's decisions and choices to pursue leadership positions (or not). Existing research highlights that family responsibilities can deter women from pursuing career advancement and senior leadership positions (Sandberg, 2013; Ward & Wolf-Wendel, 2012). Existing forecasts for gender equity in senior levels of leadership suggest that more women as faculty will translate to more women as administrators, yet the findings from our research and that of others (e.g., Hart, 2016) suggest that the choices women make throughout their careers and the culture and demands of senior leadership are not of interest to many women as they progress in their careers. As the findings suggest, the lack of movement into leadership is a matter of individual choice. The choices, however, are also shaped by the culture and context of what it means to be a leader, a topic to which we now turn.

Analysis of Women's Choices

The goal of this chapter has been to look more critically at the notion that community colleges are "good" places to work and represent "good" choices for women wanting to maintain work and family life. We offer a critical lens perspective not as a way to criticize or question individual choices; instead, the intent is to use feminist perspectives as a way to look at career choices and overall implications for community colleges as organizations striving for gender equity. The findings from the study indicate that participants are making a conscious and deliberate choice to work in community colleges, a commitment they maintain throughout the career. Community colleges are sure to benefit from such a dedicated workforce.

The findings from the study reveal that community colleges are in many ways a true success story of women and men having access to faculty and leadership positions and taking advantage of them. From a liberal feminist perspective, opportunities are available and women generally see they are able to participate fully in academic life. Parity for women has been particularly present in the faculty and student ranks (although still limited in particular disciplines). In contrast, from a poststructural feminist perspective, a key component of women choosing to work in community colleges is tied to their not wanting to work in other academic settings. In essence they are making a reactive choice to what they do *not* want (i.e., settings of publish or perish) and see community colleges as a good place to focus on what they do want (i.e., integrated lives, focus on students). Individual choice is often situated as autonomous action and not a choice that takes place in light of external influence or context (Gill, 2007). But, feminist perspectives call for looking at individual choices as well as the structure and context in which the choices are made (Thayer-Bacon et al., 2013).

Community colleges are feminized work spaces that allow faculty members to find balance between work and family. Again, these are all good things, but deeper analysis is warranted because there is still segregation by discipline and position. Just as community colleges can have a "cooling out" function for students (the notion that community colleges are places where students can opt to "cool out" in community colleges instead of transferring to 4-year institutions; Clark, 1980), the same can happen with faculty (especially women faculty). One may ask—is the choice made to work as a community college faculty member akin to the decision by a student to attend a community college rather than a 4-year institution? Does the community college serve a cooling-out function for faculty members—diverting some who might be successful at a 4-year institution to opt out because they believe the community college to be less stressful and less demanding? Is the community college setting cooling out potential leaders, as women faculty members decide not to become administrators? To be sure, not all faculty are destined for 4-year universities or top administrative positions; the point here is that the choices people make to work in particular settings can be confounded by the environment and perceptions of the environment. Choice needs to be considered not just as individual action but as a decision that takes place bounded by a set of organization norms that shape what it means to be a good professor and societal norms that dictate what it means to be a good mother (Gill, 2007; Ward & Wolf-Wendel, 2012).

The challenge remains: How can colleges and universities, including 2-year institutions, reconcile the challenges women still face in the workplace as professors and at home as mothers? The response is twofold. First, colleges can shift the focus from individual women and their choices to the larger institutional influences that include structural rules and polices in which women make such choices. Second, college leaders can consider alternative perspectives regarding academic careers as well as critique and provide solutions that more fully consider the roles of men and women in colleges and at home (and how the two interact) that shape workplace realities.

Given all the attention campuses and individuals are dedicating to how to create integration between work and family, it would seem that women would be making considerable progress in breaking the motherhood glass ceiling and transcending motherhood penalties. Yet the compendium of existing research suggests that academic women continue to be limited in their progress to the most senior levels—even at community colleges that offer more accommodations. In particular, many women in our study rejected promotion to senior administrative roles and instead opted to remain a regular faculty member until they retire. To move women into leadership requires an examination of individual choice and the context in which the choice is made. It also requires looking at workplace norms that make women feel they can and cannot do certain things based on gendered norms and expectations.

Conclusion

The leadership crisis in community colleges has led to speculation on who will lead these colleges in the future and how best to prepare leaders for leadership positions. There is heightened concern about leadership succession in community colleges given high rates of turnover and retirements (Mackey, 2008). It is important to look at faculty career trajectories to understand why more women faculty reject opportunities in administration. It is particularly important to look at faculty who are midcareer and established because this is the cohort that is poised and experienced to transition into senior leadership (Hart, 2016). There has been little research about faculty members already in community colleges and their career progression despite the fact that the majority of presidents come from within community colleges and that midlevel administrators and midcareer faculty show little interest to move into senior-level administrator positions (Garza Mitchell & Eddy, 2008). In line with the purposes of this volume to consider the positionality and place of gender and women in community colleges, it is important to look at career trajectories, individual choices, and structural realities that lead to faculty members becoming institutional leaders. If the goal is to create greater parity and equity for women in all levels of colleges and universities, including senior-level positions, it is important to guide future practice in community colleges that shape leadership development, policy revision, and mentorship in an effort to help address leadership shortages and to remedy gender gaps in leadership.

References

Acker, J. (1987). Feminist theory and the study of gender and education. *International Review of Education, 33*(4), 419–435.

Allan, E. (2011). Women's status in higher education: Equity matters. [*ASHE Higher Education Report, 37*(1)]. San Francisco, CA: Jossey-Bass.

Allan, E. J., Iverson, S., & Ropers-Huilman, R. (Eds.). (2009). *Reconstructing policy in higher education: Feminist poststructural perspectives.* New York, NY: Routledge.

American Council on Education. (2012). *The American college president: 2012.* Washington, DC: Author.

Baca Zinn, M. (2000). Feminism and family studies for a new century. *Annals of the American Academy Political and Social Sciences, 571,* 42–56. Thousand Oaks, CA: Sage.

Chronicle of Higher Education. (2015). *Almanac of higher education.* http://www.chronicle.com/section/Almanac-of-Higher-Education/883

Clark, B. (1980). The "cooling out" function revisited. In G. B. Vaughan (Ed.), *New Directions for Community Colleges: No. 32. Questioning the community college role* (pp. 15–31). San Francisco, CA: Jossey Bass.

Donovan, J. (2012). *Feminist theory: The intellectual traditions* (4th ed.). New York, NY: Bloomsbury Publishing.

Drake, E. (2008). Literature conceptualizing women in community colleges: 1997–2007. *Community College Journal of Research and Practice, 32,* 762–777.

Ferguson, A. (1997). Moral responsibility and social change: A new theory of self. *Hypatia, 12,* 116–141.

Garza Mitchell, R. L., & Eddy, P. L. (2008). In the middle: A gendered view of career pathways of mid-level community college leaders. *Community College Journal of Research and Practice, 32*(10), 793–811.

Gill, R. (2007). Critical respect: The difficulties and dilemmas of agency and "choice" for feminism. *European Journal of Women's Studies, 14,* 69–80.

Hart, J. (2016). Dissecting a gendered organization: Implications for career trajectories for mid-career faculty women in STEM. *Journal of Higher Education, 87,* 605–634.

Kezar, A. J., & Sam, C. (2010). Understanding the new majority of non-tenure track faculty in higher education: Demographics, experiences, and plans of action. [*ASHE Higher Education Report Series, 36*(4)]. San Francisco, CA: Jossey-Bass.

Leslie, D. W. (2006). *Policy brief: Faculty careers and flexible employment.* New York, NY: TIAA-CREF Institute. Retrieved from https://www.tiaadirect.com/public/pdf/institute/pdf/pol010106.pdf

Lester, J. (2008). Performing gender in the workplace: Gender socialization, power, and identity among women faculty members. *Community College Review, 35,* 277–305.

Lester, J., & Sallee, M. (Eds.). (2009). *Establishing the family-friendly campus: Models for effective practice.* Sterling, VA: Stylus Publishing.

Mackey, J. A. (2008). *Community college leadership succession: Perceptions and plans of community college leaders* (Unpublished doctoral dissertation). Northern Arizona University, Flagstaff.

Mason, M., Wolfinger, N. H., & Goulden, M. (2013). *Do babies matter: Gender and family in the ivory tower.* New Brunswick, NJ: Rutgers University Press.

Perna, L. W. (2001).The relationship between family responsibilities and employment status. *Journal of Higher Education, 72*(5), 584–611.

Sallee, M. W. (2013). Gender norms and institutional culture: The family-friendly versus the father-friendly university. *Journal of Higher Education, 84*(3), 363–396.

Sandberg, S. (2013). *Lean in: Women, work and the will to leave.* New York, NY: Knopf.

Thayer-Bacon, B. J., Stone, L., & Sprecher, K. M. (2013). *Education feminism: Classic and contemporary readings.* Albany, NY: State University of New York Press.

Trower, C. (2010). A new generation of faculty: Similar core values in a different world. *Peer Review, 12,* 27–30.

Twombly, S., & Townsend, B. (2008). Community college faculty: What we need to know. *Community College Review, 36*(1), 5–24.

Ward, K., & Wolf-Wendel, L. E. (2012). *Academic motherhood: Managing work and family.* New Brunswick, NJ: Rutgers University Press.

Wolf-Wendel, L., Ward, K., & Twombly, S. (2007). Faculty life at community colleges: The perspective of women with children. *Community College Review, 34,* 255–281.

KELLY WARD *is a professor of higher education and chair of Educational Leadership, Sport Studies & Counseling/Educational Psychology at Washington State University.*

LISA WOLF-WENDEL *is a professor of higher education in the Department of Educational Leadership and Policy Studies at the University of Kansas. She is also the associate dean for research and graduate studies in the School of Education at KU.*

NEW DIRECTIONS FOR COMMUNITY COLLEGES • DOI: 10.1002/cc

5

This chapter provides a summary of the history of the Clery Act and reviews the latest developments of the Violence Against Women Reauthorization Act. In light of this legislation, campus collaboration should occur to ensure students' safety and institutional legal compliance regarding mandatory reporting requirements.

The Clery Act on Campus: Status Update and Gender Implications

E. Ashleigh Schuller Lee

The Crime Awareness and Campus Security Act of 1990 was important and timely higher education legislation that remains critical today. In 1998 the name of the original 1990 law was changed, and this updated legislation is now referred to as the Jeanne Clery Disclosure of Campus Security Policy and Campus Crime Statistics Act (Clery Act; Nobles, Fox, Khey, & Lizotte, 2013). The Clery Act obliges colleges and universities to acquire and publish campus crime statistics for the "preceding 3 years," which are defined as calendar years (Nobles et al., 2013, p. 1132; Violence Against Women Reauthorization Act of 2013 [VAWA]). The U.S. Department of Education oversees the compliance aspect of the Clery Act (Richart, 2015).

This chapter provides a literature review that critiques and reports on current updates to the Clery Act. In particular, I discuss the need for administrative collaboration among colleges and universities with respect to the Clery Act. The chapter concludes by raising questions regarding the gender implications surrounding the legislative amendments to the Clery Act. As constructions of gender have changed over time, it is critical to understand more about how laws and legislation reflect protection of individuals across the gender spectrum.

A review of the nearly 30-year history of the Clery Act provides the backdrop for the current legislation. The Clery Act is found in the updated Higher Education Act (HEA) of 1965 section 485(f) (U.S. Department of Education, 2016). The Clery Act was enacted as Title II of the Student Right-to-Know and Campus Security Act of 1990 and amended five times (1992, 1998, 2000, 2008, and 2013; U.S. Department of Education, 2016).

New Directions for Community Colleges, no. 179, Fall 2017 © 2017 Wiley Periodicals, Inc.
Published online in Wiley Online Library (wileyonlinelibrary.com) • DOI: 10.1002/cc.20262

Currently, the Clery Act is awaiting congressional action as a bill is pending with additional amendments ("Proposed Clery Act Amendments Increase Safety Procedures," 2015). The act received its current name in the 1998 amendments in honor of a female college student, Jeanne Clery, who was killed in her dorm room (U.S. Department of Education, 2016). These amendments required institutions of higher education to report their crime data annually to the U.S. Department of Education, and further amendments in 2000 required colleges and universities to provide information on the location of the state's public sex offender registry. Further, the Higher Education Opportunity Act of 2008 added the requirement of developing and distributing immediate campus emergency response and evaluation procedures. Critical to emerging gender constructions, this change required institutions to report bias-related hate crimes in four new categories: larceny, simple assault, intimidation, and destruction/damage/vandalism of property.

The most recent amendments to the Clery Act occurred in 2013 (U.S. Department of Education, 2016). These amendments are housed within the VAWA (Public Law 113–14; U.S. Department of Education, 2016). The Clery Act (also known as Title II of Public Law 101–542) requires all institutions, including community colleges and public and private 4-year institutions receiving financial aid assistance, to report crime statistics on an annual basis (U.S. Department of Education, 2016). As discussed later, the crime statistics that are mandatory to report have recently changed. If institutions do not comply with Clery Act reporting requirements, they may face tough financial penalties ("Higher Ed Institutions," 2013. For example, Virginia Tech was fined $55,000 for failing to report an active shooter on its campus in 2007 (Richart, 2015).

A discussion about Title IX helps situate the Clery Act amendments. Both Title IX and the Clery Act work together to inform authorities about crimes involving sexual violence. Broadly speaking, Title IX, which became federal law in 1972, is a general law about equity—equity and fair treatment for women in higher education (Anderson, 2016). The Clery Act, which came after Title IX, also seeks to inform the discussion surrounding gender equity, but the Clery Act narrows the focus by specifically addressing the public aspect of campus crimes through its mandatory reporting requirements. The Clery Act seeks to protect students and the campus community against perpetuated violence by making the public aware of crimes that have occurred on the campus or surrounding areas close to the campus.

First, it is important to understand how far the Clery Act has come by examining a timeline of its developments and history (see historic outline above). Important changes have been made to the Clery Act that require all institutions to be on alert to ensure they are following proper procedures. The 2015 changes to the Clery Act included a full list of the crimes for which institutions must provide a record when reporting annual crime statistics and details as to the new crimes that colleges and universities must keep track of in accordance with the 2015 law. Moreover, there are guidelines as to how a student's proceeding should be conducted when another student brings a charge of sexual assault. For example, institutions must maintain statistics about the number of incidents of dating violence, domestic violence, sexual assault, and stalking that meet the definitions of those terms. Precise definitions are now required for awareness programs, bystander intervention, prevention programs, and risk reduction. These protections now cover a wider span of gender identity instead of being limited to women.

Within the United States Code, there are several crimes outlined in the Clery Act. The initial Clery Act did not include as extensive a listing of crimes compared to the latest amendment. Three new crimes are included in the updated reporting requirements: domestic violence, dating violence, and stalking. Gardella and colleagues (2015) state:

> The Clery Act enumerates murder, sex offenses (forcible or non-forcible), robbery, aggravated assault, burglary, motor vehicle theft, manslaughter, arson, liquor law violations, drug-related violations, and weapons possessions as reportable offenses (20 USCS 1092 (f)(F)(i), 2012). Also included are larceny-theft; simple assault; intimidation; destruction, damage, or vandalism of property; and other crimes involving bodily injury on race, gender, religion, sexual orientation, ethnicity, or disability. (20 USCS 1092 (f)(F)(ii), 2012, p. 642)

The biggest changes that the VAWA made to the Clery Act involved the annual reporting of new crimes (Higher Ed Institutions, 2013). The Federal Register stated, "Notably, VAWA amended the Clery Act to require institutions to compile statistics for incidents of dating violence, domestic violence, sexual assault, and stalking and to include certain policies, procedures, and programs pertaining to these incidents in their annual security reports" (VAWA, 2014, n.p.). Because the new crimes were added and enumerated to the Clery Act, all colleges and universities should have incorporated these changes into their policies as of July 1, 2015 (VAWA, 2014). One of the keys to ensuring proper implementation of the act on campus is adequate cooperation among college offices to assure compliance with all aspects of the legislation. The updates have added additional responsibilities for school communities and serve as another reminder that the Clery Act is gaining momentum as an important issue on college campuses.

The following section reviews the Clery Act requirements, particularly as related to community colleges. Central to this literature review is a summary of the reporting requirements for colleges and universities, with attention to differences noted for community colleges. The overview critiques the Clery Act and calls for college collaboration for successful implementation of the changes in the act.

Background

All colleges and universities must comply with the Clery Act to receive federal student financial aid per Title IV (Mills-Senn, 2013;Richart, 2015; U.S. Department of Education, 2016). Thus, the Clery Act is an important carrot used to motivate public universities and colleges if they want to receive federal aid. Within the literature, there is scant information pertaining specifically to community colleges and the Clery Act. As a whole, the discussion surrounding the Clery Act is general and broadly applied to higher education as a sector. All institutions must be in compliance or else they risk paying fees to the government.

A brief review of community college websites highlights that the required reporting statistics appear present. Upon request, students, staff, and members of the public may receive hard copies of the college's annual report and statistics. Each community college (and institution of higher education) has different reporting formats, albeit as mentioned, all must comply with the required annual reporting of crime statistics. Additionally, there are reports relating to fire safety, inclement weather warnings, and missing person protocol and timelines. There are several requirements embedded within the Clery Act with which all community colleges and universities must comply (U.S. Department of Education, 2016). Importantly, among the amendments to the Clery Act in 2013 (as previously discussed) are new requirements for reporting dating violence and stalking (U.S. Department of Education, 2016).

No reporting agency or process is without its flaws. The Clery Act is no exception. Despite the scant research on crime and the Clery Act on college and university campuses, one critique made surrounds the manner in which the crime statistics are collected (Nobles et al., 2013). For example,

> From a methodological standpoint, there are concerns about accuracy and reliability stemming from the tabulation of what is ostensibly "campus crime." For example, data to satisfy the Clery Act requirements are collected by campus law enforcement agencies and, consequently, only reflect crimes known to the police. This method of data collection is subject to agency reporting problems and the hierarchy rule (meaning only the most serious of a series of crimes by one offender is recorded), similar to the Uniform Crime Reports (UCR). While most prior research has examined campus crime and college student criminality through the use of self-report data on offending, researchers have largely avoided official college crime reports at the aggregate level (e.g., police arrest data). Thus, from a research standpoint, the use of official data in this capacity has been incomplete. (Nobles et al., 2013, p. 1132)

Thus, although the Clery Act reports crime among other data, the method in which the data are reported and conveyed to the public may remain open for interpretation. More studies need to be conducted regarding the reporting system's integrity and accuracy.

In addition to these shortcomings within the Clery Act reporting system, the study by Nobles and colleagues (2013) also discusses the need to understand where campus crime occurs when reporting the statistics and how knowing whether the crime is being committed on or off campus matters in terms of reporting accurate information to interested students and their families. These shortcomings continue to highlight the need for all facets of the campus community to come together to share information.

Moreover, another concern regarding community colleges lies in the limited resources that the campus communities, in particular adjunct faculty, are privy to in terms of threat assessment and students of concern (Bennett & Bates, 2015). The profile of students attending community colleges often looks different from that of a 4-year university college student in terms of age, work status, and campus extracurricular involvement (Bennett & Bates, 2015). Oftentimes, students who have been dismissed from a 4-year university because of discipline infractions or having committed a crime as defined by the Clery Act are able to enroll in a community college through open admission policies (Bennett & Bates, 2015). For community colleges, there is an even greater imperative to collaborate with universities or other, more resourced community colleges to ensure campus safety is not compromised (Bennett & Bates, 2015).

Recently, a senator from Missouri has championed the need for the Clery Act to become more streamlined and less burdensome on campus staff in terms of paperwork (Richart, 2015). Senator Claire McCaskill addressed the Campus Safety National Forum in Washington, DC and made bold statements that the Clery Act is unworkable and too difficult for colleges and universities to comply with (Richart). "The rhetoric about abandoning the Clery Act suggests that a tipping point has been reached and a critical mass of campus public safety personnel are effectively fed up with the onus of the reporting requirements" (Richart, para. 8). This final critique addresses the bottom line dilemma that the Clery Act is imperfect but important. A team approach to effectively and efficiently enforce the act remains critical. First, interinstitutional communication is required given how much students swirl enrollment among colleges. A student infraction at one college may not be documented upon enrollment in a new college. Second, intrainstitutional coordination is required to support the work of multiple offices charged with protecting the well-being of students against gender violence.

Moving Forward

The literature highlights the need for colleges and universities to focus on a collaborative nature to meet the compliance requirements (Mills-Senn, 2013). For example, because the Clery Act requires colleges and universities to report both the nature and the frequency of the crime, the process can be onerous (Mills-Senn). However, the stakes are extremely high if a college or university omits a crime in its annual report. The Department of Education fines the college or university $35,000 for each infraction (Mills-Senn). Additionally, some colleges and universities with reporting problems have been put on notice and more will follow (Mills-Senn).

In order to comply with the Clery Act, all institutions of higher education must maintain a daily crime log, along with a fire log (U.S. Department of Education, 2016). The Clery Act statistics are to be reported annually with disclosure of the statistics available to the public (U.S. Department of Education, 2016). A recent quantitative study conducted by researchers at Virginia Tech highlighted yet another concern that victim advocates expressed in their study regarding the reporting requirement of the Clery Act: "A paradox that advocates often experience is an increase in the number of reports of crime due to increased educational efforts, not because the rate of crime increases" (Janosik & Plummer, 2005, p. 127). Higher crime reporting numbers may reflect heightened awareness and better reporting of infractions on campus that had previously gone unreported. These spikes, however, do not always represent the occurrence of more crimes, but public fear about campus safety may ratchet up.

Agencies must and should work together to meet the requirements of the Clery Act. Police and other safety personnel must have the financial support and commitment from college leadership in order to effectively comply with the Clery Act (Whissemore, 2015). More resources, time, and effort are being spent ensuring community colleges can meet the Clery Act's requirements and recent updates (Whissemore). Yet, scarce resources may result in less institutional compliance with the Clery Act (Whissemore). Based on the literature, financial resources contribute to a college successfully addressing the recent changes to the Clery Act.

Within the discussion and literature surrounding the Clery Act, there is research on victimization among college women (Gardella et al., 2015). Much of the existing research on the Clery Act has surrounded rape, stalking, harassment, and sexual conduct, and women are typically the subjects of these studies (Gardella et al.). Yet, for the rest of the crimes outlined within the Clery Act, little study occurs (Gardella et al.). However, in light of the recent amendments to the Clery Act, hate crimes are now enumerated, as well as a distinction between gender and national origin (VAWA, 2014). Given the distinction between gender and national origin, speculation is that more men and transgender students may come forward to report crimes. Before the amendments were added, the focus of the Clery Act was predominantly on women and crimes against women.

Now, as we move into 2017 and beyond, colleges and universities have a broader focus and more defined categories of crime prevention and education. Because the legal language is nuanced given the recent amendments, there should be a deeper understanding given to specific groups of

NEW DIRECTIONS FOR COMMUNITY COLLEGES • DOI: 10.1002/cc

individuals who are victims of crimes Thus, the need for campus administrators, faculty, students, and college employees to more fully understand the literature surrounding victimization and gender distinctions remains important to encouraging more victims to report crimes and ultimately to prevent crimes.

Even with the new legislation and categories, the Clery Act has not dramatically changed college students' reporting of violent crimes. Given the low national reporting average in terms of sexual assault, research shows that college students report even less than the national average (Mancini, Pickett, Call, & Roche, 2016). Moreover, victims report that they do not turn in their offenders because of concern for what the offender may do to them (Mancini et al., 2016; Pérez & Hussey, 2014). Given the societal stigma, the perception of being a victim must change if the Clery Act is to continue to be a successful deterrent to campus-related crimes. If victims are not coming forward to report crimes, then the Clery Act will not be able to accurately portray college campus crime rates.

Without further research and studies regarding the particular victimization experienced by such factors as race and gender, gaps remain in the literature surrounding the Clery Act (Gardella et al., 2015). As a society, we must change the environment in order to encourage more college students to report crimes. In order to change the environment, the college campus culture must change too. The narrow focus on crimes against women must broaden to include males as well as students with different sexual orientations (Pérez & Hussey, 2014). Anyone can become a victim, but everyone has the power to come together to change the perception of society regarding crimes against students on campus. Collaboration among campus units is key in order to empower all campus stakeholders and the families of community college students to reach out if they are concerned for another person's safety.

The Clery Act, as a living and malleable piece of federal legislation, will continue to grow in scope and application. Community college leaders must keep abreast of the dramatic changes and enhancements or risk being noncompliant. With student safety in the balance, increased attention to supporting easy reporting, providing educational training for staff and faculty, and preventing crime is imperative.

References

Anderson, M. J. (2016). Campus sexual assault adjudication and resistance to reform. *Yale Law Journal*, 125(7). Retrieved from https://ssrn.com/abstract=2767058

Bennett, L., & Bates, M. (2015). Threat assessment and targeted violence at institutions of higher education: Implications for policy and practice including unique considerations for community colleges. *JEP: Ejournal of Education Policy*, 1–16.

Gardella, J. H., Nichols-Hadeed, C. A., Mastrocinque, J. M., Stone, J. T., Coates, C. A., Sly, C. J., & Cerulli, C. (2015). Beyond Clery Act statistics: A closer look at college

NEW DIRECTIONS FOR COMMUNITY COLLEGES • DOI: 10.1002/cc

victimization based on self-report data. *Journal of Interpersonal Violence, 30*(4), 640–658. https://doi.org/10.1177/0886260514535257

Higher ed institutions face Title IX complaints. (2013). *Campus Legal Advisor, 13*(11), 2.

Janosik, S. M., & Plummer, E. (2005). The Clery Act, campus safety and the views of assault victim advocates. *College Student Affairs Journal, 25*(1), 116–130.

Jeanne Clery Disclosure of Campus Security Policy and Campus Crime Statistics Act. 20 U.S.C. § 1092(f).

Mancini, C., Pickett, J., Call, C., & Roche, S. P. (2016). Mandatory reporting (MR) in higher education: College students' perception of laws designed to reduce campus sexual assault. *Criminal Justice Review, 41*(2), 219–235.

Mills-Senn, P. (2013). Taking control of Clery Act compliance. *University Business, 16*(8), 26–29.

Nobles, M. R., Fox, K. A., Khey, D. N., & Lizotte, A. J. (2013). Community and campus crime: A geospatial examination of the Clery Act. *Crime & Delinquency, 59*(8), 1131–1156. https://doi.org/10.1177/0011128710372188

Pérez, Z. J., & Hussey, H. (2014). *A hidden crisis: Including the LGBT community when addressing sexual violence on college campuses.* Washington, DC: Center for American Progress.

Proposed Clery Act amendments increase safety procedures. (2015). *Campus Security Report, 12*(3), 12.

Richart, A. (2015). Reporting rules undermine Clery Act goals: Lifting burdens would help law enforcement keep campuses safe. *Community College Week, 27*(26), 38.

Title IX, Education Amendments of 1972. Title 20 U.S.C. Sections 1681–1688.

U.S. Department of Education, Office of Postsecondary Education. (2016). *The handbook for campus safety and security reporting,* 2016 Edition. Washington, DC: Author.

Violence Against Women Act. (2014, Oct. 20). Federal Register. Retrieved from https://www.federalregister.gov/documents/2014/10/20/2014-24284/violence-against-women-act

Whissemore, T. (2015). Clery Act changes the landscape of campus safety. *Community College Journal, 86*(3), 4–5.

E. ASHLEIGH SCHULLER LEE, JD, PhD, *is an adjunct professor at the College of William & Mary in Williamsburg, Virginia.*

NEW DIRECTIONS FOR COMMUNITY COLLEGES • DOI: 10.1002/cc

6

This chapter reports on three research studies conducted by the Center for Research on Educational Access and Leadership (C-REAL) at California State University, Fullerton (CSUF) that are designed to help higher education institutions enhance their practices in serving men of color, namely Black and Latino men.

The Intersectionality of Gender and Race—Programs to Support Men of Color in Education

Dawn Person, Robert Dawson, Yvonne García, Andrew Jones

Community colleges are the most viable and often the only possible option to access higher education for many men of color (Center for Community College Student Engagement, 2014). Even though community colleges are perceived as nimble by necessity, the institutional response to persistence and graduation for men of color is an area of limited institutional change. Much of what is written about men of color focuses primarily on their needs specific to academic support, with some attention to culture (Lewis & Middleton, 2003). Beyond race, there are issues of gender, and beyond gender there are issues of race. Yet, little research considers the intersection of race and gender (Hondagneu-Sotelo, Zinn, & Denissen, 2015). This point of intersection of the two constructs highlights the most critical aspects of serving and supporting this population. Identity formation occurs in this intersection and includes both what it means to be male and what it means to be a man of color (Hondagneu-Sotelo et al., 2015). The complexity of male gender and racial/ethnic identity is explored in this chapter, along with best practices to support men of color, their identity development, and academic success in community college settings.

Men of color have different experiences on community college campuses compared to women of color and White men and women. For example, being White and male includes a historically privileged existence that may at first seem transferable to non-White men based on gender. But, men of color face an imposed wall based on race that counters gender privilege. In the end, men of color do not garner the privilege typically conferred to

NEW DIRECTIONS FOR COMMUNITY COLLEGES, no. 179, Fall 2017 © 2017 Wiley Periodicals, Inc.
Published online in Wiley Online Library (wileyonlinelibrary.com) • DOI: 10.1002/cc.20263

men; rather, it is an illusion or a myth for these men. This finding makes it critical to consider the experiences of men of color including their voices in both the literature and support systems at community colleges.

Literature Review

Community colleges are the primary pathways for African Americans and Latinos to pursue postsecondary education (American Association of Community Colleges [AACC], 2016; Lewis & Middleton, 2003). African American and Latino males at community colleges have not experienced the same success as other racial/ethnic and gender groups. Nationally, about half of Latinos and a third of African American students start at a community college, whereas only about a quarter of White students begin at community colleges (National Center for Public Policy and Higher Education, 2011). Yet, White students achieve success at higher rates with 59% attaining an associate degree or higher compared to only 15% of Latinos and 12% of African Americans (AACC, 2016). Student success gaps are even more prevalent when looking at the achievement rates of men of color. In each ethnic group, young women outperform men in high school and higher education attainment rates. To understand this achievement imbalance between genders requires an examination of how intersecting identities related to race and privilege (or lack thereof) play out in the lives of men of color.

The kinds of skill and social capital that Black and Latino men come into the education system with are typically not valued or recognized by the traditional norms of higher education. Community colleges and other sectors of higher education serve men of color from a deficit model perspective, not considering the strengths and assets they brought to the college experience (Harper, 2008). In addition to institutional devaluing of men of color, Black and Latino men are presented with many challenges in continuing and completing an associate degree such as financial instability, academic unpreparedness, and consistently combating negative stereotypes (Wood, 2012). Resiliency provides individuals a way to rebound from stressful events or difficult situations and is based on both internal and external characteristics that allow them to thrive (Jones, Higgins, Brandon, Cote, & Dobbins, 2013). Jones and Person (2016) and Person (2016) described the resiliency characteristics of successful Black and Latino men as high achievers with extraordinary aspirations who were motivated and overcame numerous difficulties. Resiliency is evident for men of color who are successful in navigating postsecondary education given the small percentage who complete their degrees (Wood, 2012).

Pivotal to understanding the college learning experience for men of color is the reorientation of racial/ethnic identity consciousness. Here, it is critical to move beyond the racial/ethnic development of Black and Latino men by also considering how their academic development contributes to their college success. As such, habits of mind (HoM) are important skills that contribute to successful behaviors in college students, facilitating engagement in the classroom and developing social-emotional skills (Bernard, 2006). Central to the engagement of Black and Latino men, HoM are important skills that include being able to ask for help, working with peers, setting goals, and developing critical thinking skills. For example, men who are able to connect with positive role models and receive mentoring support services are able to enhance faculty–student relationships, which leads to improvement in student success and retention (LaVant, Anderson, & Tiggs, 1997).

The element of race is often discussed when considering success for men of color but rarely the intersection of race and gender specific to the community college setting. This chapter helps fill this void by investigating the intersection of race and gender for Black and Latino men in community colleges and also describing best practices for student support.

Research Background

This chapter incorporates findings from three different research studies of community college students that include two campus-based case studies and a national study:

1. The first is a longitudinal case study of a campuswide intervention that examined the effect of a student success initiative involving Latino men (iFALCON) that was implemented at Cerritos College in Norwalk, California from 2009–2014. This intervention focused on the campus culture shifting to incorporate habits of mind into the campus curricular and cocurricular activities, and support services.
2. The second is a case study of a student success initiative at Los Angeles Southwest College in Los Angeles, California, designed to increase retention and engagement for African American men. The Passage intervention provided academic, cultural, and financial support to African American and Latino men and offered them a support network to assist in their transition into college. Additionally, instructional support was provided in the classroom and through supplemental instruction.
3. The third study is a national longitudinal study of participants involved in campus-based Minority Male Initiatives (MMIs) who attended a Men of Color Leadership Institute (MOCLI) coordinated by the Presidents' Round Table, a national network of African American community college chief executive officers. These high-achieving men engaged in a 3-day motivational and life planning program for success with other Black and Latino men across the country. They shared their perspectives on the college-going experience based on their campus site including the role and function of the MMI.

New Directions for Community Colleges • DOI: 10.1002/cc

MMI is an intensive intervention designed to specifically meet the needs of men of color in community college settings.

Findings

Black and Latino men across the different projects reported benefitting from culturally responsive support systems facilitated through MMI programs that helped them develop critical academic skills while also becoming more connected to their colleges. Specifically, the MOCLI participants highlighted how their motivation to be successful and serve as a role model for others contributed to their drive to succeed. Men from the iFALCON program noted how they used HoM skills. What follows is a synthesis of qualitative and quantitative data findings from the three studies.

Resiliency and Motivations to Pursue Higher Education. The men in the 2014–2016 MOCLI study were surveyed about their resiliency and were asked about the challenges they faced inside and outside the classroom, along with what motivated them to persist through challenges. The top challenges identified by the participants were financial (66.7%, $n = 56$), family (39.3%, $n = 33$), academics (36.9%, $n = 31$), and interacting with peers (29.8%, $n = 25$). Another challenge for some students involved the stigma around mental health issues; about 9% ($n = 18$) of participants reported also having some kind of learning disability. Participants from the Passage program expressed similar challenges inside and outside the classroom during the focus groups; students talked about issues with finances and affording college, finding adequate study spaces outside of school, and balancing the responsibilities of school and work.

Many men were motivated to be successful in college to improve their lives and the lives of individuals around them, while also working to serve as a positive role model to their family and ethnic communities. As one participant commented about being an example for younger men: "become a leader, somebody you can look up to at the end of the day." Men from the MOCLI cited their families as strong motivators to pursue higher education. One young man from the MOCLI explained that "failure is not an option at all. I want a better life than I've had and [that] my family has had… most of my life." Many of the men participating in the MOCLI reported their motivations to pursue higher education included the desire to have a better life (76.8%, $n = 63$), desire to help others (56.6%, $n = 47$), and serving as a role model for others (56.6%, $n = 47$).

The participants from the Passage program provided similar reasoning to pursue higher education. One young man explained his conflict as "I want to go higher and attain a PhD, but [I] have to worry about [my] family as well. I have to go back and take care of them." Participants were in agreement that the option of college was a way to pursue greater income and opportunities, along with providing a sense of security and providing for their families. Data collected over the course of the 5 years of the

MOCLI program showed that the men maintained their goals to pursue a bachelor's degree or higher, contrary to the cooling-out effect traditionally associated with community colleges. iFALCON program participants also reported high aspirations in terms of educational goals. Specifically, 80% expected to transfer or complete their degree at Cerrito College, and fewer than 5% expected to earn a certificate, whereas 95% expected to earn a minimum of an associate's degree. Additionally, 41% anticipated completing a bachelor's degree and almost 20% also planned to complete a postgraduate degree.

Student Engagement.   The men who participated in MOCLI and Passage reported engagement with their colleges. The men from MOCLI indicated that the most common forms of engagement occurred with peers/friends or the tutoring and counseling offices. Participants reported using peers/friends *often* (46.7%, $n = 92$), counseling (34.2%, $n = 68$), and tutoring (33.2%, $n = 66$) as resources. The least used resources reported by students were disabled and veteran student services as well as supplemental instruction. In addition, the men from Passage said tutoring services provided to them were "keys to the success" of the program. Students indicated that both the group and individual tutoring was helpful, but noted that the individual tutoring was more effective (70.3%, $n = 26$) compared to the group tutoring (59.5%, $n = 22$). Most students reported that the weekly tutoring sessions were either *effective* (43.2%, $n = 16$) or *very effective* (21.6%, $n = 8$).

Similar to the testimonies from men in the MOCLI, participants in Passage appreciated the brotherhood that developed within the program. One student explained "I know I have my brothers in there with me." This cohesion was also noticed by faculty members who worked with the program. Faculty noticed students forming bonds as well as holding each other accountable for their classwork. Men engaged with peers from similar backgrounds, which facilitated the development of genuine and sincere bonds. The group also developed a strong sense of brotherhood that allowed students to bond over shared experiences. These findings support the notion that these men needed to be formally and informally engaged with their academic institutions, but they also greatly benefitted from having shared spaces with their peers.

Although student engagement is a multidimensional construct critical for students' success, aggregate findings from these studies support the idea that high-achieving students were more engaged. For example, students at Cerritos College were exposed to and encouraged to use HoM behaviors in and outside of the classroom in order to enhance critical academic skills, as well as facilitate interactions with peers, faculty, and staff via the iFALCON intervention. Based on survey findings, students that reported using more HoM skills also reported higher rates of academic confidence, as well as higher grade point averages (GPAs). Students also reported using specific HoM skills more often than others, specifically, understanding the importance of attending all class sessions, being responsible for their learning, and being focused on school work.

School Involvement. One common element across two of the projects was campus organizations designed for men of color. The men participating in MMI programming discussed the importance of interacting with peers, teachers, administrators, and the educational institution as a whole. The men who participated in MOCLI shared that the organization afforded them opportunities to talk and interact with peers from similar backgrounds. This aided in their feeling more connected with campus resources. One man mentioned,

> Before joining Male Access [MMI], I didn't know how the school had these workshops for these colleges. These workshops that teach you how to apply for [scholarships], what do with the money, transferring... None of that would have shown up on my radar had I not become involved.

In addition to campus involvement, many of the men were also active in different organizations and clubs on campus, as well as working part-time or full-time jobs. Of the 149 men who reported identifying as Black or African American from the MOCLI, 72.5% ($n = 108$) were also employed (part time or full time), and many were also *very involved* (57.9%, $n = 84$) with the campus life at their school. Almost all of the 39 Hispanic or Latino men in this study were also employed while in school (92.3%, $n = 36$), and they also reported being *very involved* (69.2%, $n = 27$). Participants were involved with campus organizations and leadership positions while also balancing the responsibilities of employment. They discussed how these organizations allowed the opportunity to develop leadership skills and share them with their peers. Involvement led directly to awareness and knowledge of campus resources and personnel support available to assist men of color. For the most part, these men saw strong positive benefits from their involvement on and off campus.

Benefits of MMI Programming. Many colleges have adopted MMI programming to support student academic success by providing services including: tutoring, mentoring, advising, financial assistance, and creating environments for young men to share common experiences. Many of the men recognized that MMI programming created new ways for them to engage with their peers. Some men remained hesitant to disclose personal information or ask for help, as these actions can be perceived as a sign of weakness or insecurity, preventing many individuals from having more open conversations (Harris, Wood, & Newman, 2015). One student explained,

> We need male-male camaraderie. I see females doing it, but I don't see us doing it. What I realize is, we are so masculine in our nature we don't want to connect. Us working in this group, these are friends now, this is [family].

New Directions for Community Colleges • DOI: 10.1002/cc

The relationships and camaraderie that developed from participating in the program helped men break away from the expected stereotypical roles and gave them opportunities to collaborate and learn from one another.

The men that participated in the Passage program provided feedback on the resources provided by the program, including their perceptions around tutoring, counseling, and mentoring services. One student explained how "a mentor was impactful. I can't even describe how beneficial the mentor was more than anything." Many of the men mentioned how they highly valued the tutoring and mentoring services that were provided by Passage. One of the men added, "The camaraderie that develop in the program was also a contributing factor [to] the students' academic success." The sense of brotherhood was salient, as the men benefited from the communal and shared experiences with peers. These program settings allowed the men of color to break away from the common perceptions that they face as men of color and engage in purposeful dialogue with other men who share common experiences.

Implications

The findings from the three studies reviewed indicate a number of best practices and programming options to better support men of color in community colleges. These practices include creating spaces for men to develop camaraderie and engage in discussion, interventions that support identity development, and development as a male, including racial and ethnic identity development. Along with the benefits for identity development, many men noted benefits from mentoring services, both peer and professional. In addition, programs should intentionally provide academic support services and incorporate HoM skills, specifically to develop and practice positive academic skills sets. The findings highlighted how the use of HoM skills were associated with increased engagement and higher student GPA. Because many men had difficulty asking questions and asking for help (Vogel, Wester, Hammer, & Downing-Matibag, 2014), programs that teach and encourage these kinds of academic behaviors can result in academic success for minority men. Knowing the benefits of counseling services and peer support and the reluctance of men to ask for help, men must be taught to ask for help as needed. Attaining comfort in this component skill is critical to student success and engagement.

Another best practice to create in support programs are opportunities for networking and career development. Because many of the men who participated in the research reported high aspirations, programs should be aimed at supporting these goals through career and professional identity development. Finally, it is important for young men to understand the importance of prioritizing academic, professional, and personal responsibilities. Many of the men of color were working part-time jobs and involved with student organizations on campus. A balance must be struck between being involved and becoming overly involved given the risk of nonacademic engagement taking priority over academics.

Conclusion

The research reported in this chapter highlights how men of color navigated both their gender and race and what they identified as critical to their college success. Fully embracing race, culture, and gender identities and adapting effective HoM supported the MOCLI participants. The men who reported using more HoM skills also were more likely to have a higher grade point average, which supports previous findings that emotional regulation is connected with academic success in students (Parker, Summerfeldt, Hogan, & Majeski, 2004). The men in all three studies began to negotiate the academic culture with support from institutional agents and MMI/academic programs that valued them equally as men and as racial beings. Furthermore, this study is in alignment with previous research that has found that Black and Latino men are motivated to create more opportunities for themselves as well as pave the way for others (Harper, 2005).

These interventions provide examples of how programming can be designed to meet the unique needs of male students while also consciously addressing their experiences as men of color. To address only one of these identities does not fully embrace the complicated identities that Black and Latino men navigate each day. MMI programs allowed Black and Latino men spaces to develop a sense of brotherhood while also supporting campus connection and engagement. Their behavioral outcomes suggest that demonstrating HoM, resiliency, self-appraisal, and awareness leads to academic engagement and involvement that supports their holistic development as racial and gender beings.

References

American Association of Community Colleges. (2016). *Minority male student success in the nation's community colleges*. Washington, DC: Author. Retrieved from http://www.aacc.nche.edu/Resources/aaccprograms/diversity/Documents/MM_Page_March2016_R2.pdf

Bernard, M. E. (2006). It's time we teach social-emotional competence as well as we teach academic competence. *Reading & Writing Quarterly, 22*(2), 103–119.

Center for Community College Student Engagement. (2014). *Aspirations to achievement: Men of color and community colleges*. Austin, TX: University of Texas at Austin, Program in Higher Education Leadership.

Harper, S. R. (2005). Leading the way: Inside the experiences of high-achieving African American male students. *About Campus, 10*(1), 8–15.

Harper, S. R. (2008). Realizing the intended outcomes of Brown: High-achieving African American male undergraduates and social capital. *American Behavioral Scientist, 51*(7), 1030–1053.

Harris, F., Wood, J., & Newman, C. (2015). An exploratory investigation of the effect of racial and masculine identity on focus: An examination of White, Black, Mexicano,

Latino, and Asian men in community colleges. *Culture, Society and Masculinities*, 7(1), 61–72.

Hondagneu-Sotelo, P., Zinn, M. B., & Denissen, A. M. (2015). *Gender through the prism of difference* (4th ed.). New York, NY: Oxford University Press.

Jones, V., Higgins, K., Brandon, R., Cote, D., & Dobbins, N. (2013). A focus on resiliency. *Young Exceptional Children*, 16(4), 3–16.

Jones, V., & Person, D. (2016, May 26–28). Resiliency in action: Thriving African American men in community college settings. In K. Higgins & R. Boone (Eds.), *Building bridges: Special Education Conference II* (pp. 62–68). Nicosia, Cypress and Las Vegas, NV: University of Nicosia and University of Nevada Las Vegas.

LaVant, B. D., Anderson, J. L., & Tiggs, J. W. (1997). Retaining African American men through mentoring initiatives. In M. J. Cuyjet (Ed.), *New Directions for Student Services: No. 80. Helping African American men succeed in college* (pp. 42–53). San Francisco, CA: Jossey-Bass.

Lewis, C. W., & Middleton, V. (2003). African Americans in community colleges: A review of research reported in the community college journal of research and practice: 1990–2000. *Community College Journal of Research &Practice*, 27(9–10), 787–798.

National Center for Public Policy and Higher Education. (2011). *Affordability and transfer: Critical to increasing baccalaureate degree completion. Policy alert.* Retrieved from http://www.highereducation.org/reports/pa_at/index.shtml

Parker, J. D., Summerfeldt, L. J., Hogan, M. J., & Majeski, S. A. (2004). Emotional intelligence and academic success: Examining the transition from high school to university. *Personality and Individual Differences*, 36(1), 163–172.

Person, D. R. (2016). *Men of Color Leadership Institute summative report.* Fullerton, CA: Center for Research on Educational Access and Leadership.

Vogel, D. L., Wester, S. R., Hammer, J. H., & Downing-Matibag, T. M. (2014). Referring men to seek help: The influence of gender role conflict and stigma. *Psychology of Men & Masculinity*, 15(1), 60.

Wood, J. L. (2012). Bottom line: From the right to fail to the right to succeed: Black males in community colleges. *About Campus*, 17, 30–32. https://doi.org/10.1002/abc.21078

DAWN PERSON is a professor in the College of Education, Educational Leadership Department at California State University, Fullerton, and the director of the Center for Research on Educational Access & Leadership (C-REAL). Dawn has over 25 years of experience working in higher education, focusing on resiliency and supporting students of color.

ROBERT DAWSON is finishing a master of arts in experimental psychology at California State University, Fullerton, focusing on quantitative methods and developmental psychology. Robert was the lead research analyst for the Minority Male Initiative Database, creating a national database focusing on male student success in community colleges. Robert also coordinated the data for the iFALCON intervention at Cerritos College.

NEW DIRECTIONS FOR COMMUNITY COLLEGES • DOI: 10.1002/cc

YVONNE GARCÍA *earned a bachelor of arts in sociology and a master of science in education degree from California State University, Fullerton. Yvonne currently serves as the program coordinator for the Center for Research on Educational Access and Leadership where she oversees student researchers who conduct evaluation research on issues and programs of educational access, leadership, and success.*

ANDREW C. JONES *is a former chancellor, executive vice chancellor, and president of Coast Community College, and is now retired. He focused much of his leadership efforts in addressing the challenges of minority males and most recently serves as a member of the C-REAL advisory board.*

NEW DIRECTIONS FOR COMMUNITY COLLEGES • DOI: 10.1002/cc

7

This chapter explores the unique needs of women student–veterans and highlights the ways that community college leaders can support women student–veterans on their college campuses.

From Boots to Suits: Women Veterans Transitioning to Community College Students

Judie A. Heineman

Almost two million U.S. soldiers, sailors, air force members, and Marines have returned home from wartime service looking for new opportunities and ways to secure the future for themselves and their families (Lighthall, 2012; O'Herrin, 2011). Of these two million service members, almost 16% are women, many of whom are turning to higher education to enhance their employment prospects, expand their knowledge and skill sets, and achieve their career goals (Demers, 2013; McBain, Kim, Cook, & Snead, 2012). It is estimated that 43% of students who served in the military and who decide to attend college will do so at public 2-year institutions (Radford, 2011; Wheeler, 2012).

This chapter explores the unique needs of women student–veterans and focuses on the ways that practitioners can support these student–veterans on their college campuses. The chapter reviews the stressors faced by veterans, and by women veterans in particular, and suggests ways to provide support for these students as they transition into the community college. By being prepared to address the special needs, transition issues, challenges, and opportunities the women student–veterans bring to the college environment, college leaders can better welcome and assist this group on its campuses now and for years to come.

Stressors Faced by Women Warriors

Notwithstanding recent attention focused on the needs of student–veterans on college campuses, women student–veterans remain an understudied population (Baechtold & De Sawal, 2009; DiRamio & Jarvis, 2011;

NEW DIRECTIONS FOR COMMUNITY COLLEGES, no. 179, Fall 2017 © 2017 Wiley Periodicals, Inc.
Published online in Wiley Online Library (wileyonlinelibrary.com) • DOI: 10.1002/cc.20264

77

DiRamio, Jarvis, Iverson, Seher, & Anderson, 2015; Hamrick & Rumann, 2012). This lack of research attention is significant considering that
women make up 57% of the student population at community colleges
(American Association of Community Colleges, 2016). Previous research
was conducted on veterans, in general, without specifying gender (DiRamio
& Jarvis, 2011; Persky & Oliver, 2010; Rumann & Hamrick, 2010; Rumann,
Rivera, & Hernandez, 2011; Wheeler, 2012). As such, community colleges
may lack the tools needed to assist women student–veterans who are navigating a path from the very structured military environment to the more
open academic classrooms and campuses.

Research shows women veterans encounter many problems shared
with their nonveteran female peers, such as mental health issues, sexual assault, and the challenges associated with childcare (Baechtold & De Sawal,
2009; DiRamio et al., 2015; Mattocks et al., 2012; Street, Vogt, & Dutra,
2009). Wartime deployment has involved exposure to a range of potentially
stressful and/or traumatic experiences (Gunter-Hunt, Feldman, Gendron,
Bonney, & Unger, 2013; Street et al., 2009). The *compounding* effect of the
normal military stressors (childcare, financial concerns, personal relationships, family separation, and reunions; Baechtold & De Sawal, 2009; Mattocks et al., 2012), departure from the military, and the ensuing transition to
the community college environment warrants research exploration. Specifically, a review of posttraumatic stress disorder, military sexual trauma, interpersonal stressors, and homecoming adjustment provides a context to
understand better the challenges facing women student-veterans.

Posttraumatic Stress Disorder (PTSD). A 2010 Veterans Administration report stated that "PTSD is a recognized anxiety disorder resulting
from exposure to direct or indirect threat of death, serious injury, or a physical threat which causes a person to feel intense fear, helplessness, or hor-
ror" (U.S. Department of Veterans Affairs, 2010, p. 2). Symptoms of PTSD
can include recurrent thoughts of a traumatic event, reduced involvement
in work or outside interests, emotional numbing, hyperalertness, anxiety,
and/or irritability. The report further noted that the disorder can be more
severe and longer lasting when the stressor is a human-initiated action such
as war, rape, assault, or terrorism.

The connection between PTSD, combat exposure, and military veterans status has been acknowledged for many years, yet only limited research
has been conducted on women veterans and their ability to deal with the
effects of PTSD (Baechtold & De Sawal, 2009; DiRamio & Jarvis, 2011;
Street et al., 2009). Reports indicate that women veterans are more likely
than their male counterparts to suffer from PTSD; however, women are
not as likely to be diagnosed with PTSD as men (Baechtold & De Sawal,
2009; Gunter-Hunt et al., 2013). Scholars posit that this lack of attention
on women veterans results from cultural views that hinder acknowledging
women as combatants and the tendency to diagnose women's mental health

issues as depression or anxiety rather than PTSD (Baechtold & De Sawal, 2009; DiRamio & Jarvis, 2011).

Military Sexual Trauma (MST).   Actual and perceived combat dangers are only one type of stressor faced by women service members, as women in the military must also cope with the threat of gender-based violence before, during, and after deployment at home, overseas, or to a war zone (Mattocks et al., 2012; Murdoch et al., 2006). Military sexual trauma (MST) is the term used by the Department of Veterans Affairs to refer to sexual assault or repeated, threatening sexual harassment that occurred while the service member was in the military (Murdoch et al., 2006). At the most severe end of the spectrum is sexual assault, which could range from unwanted touching to attempted or completed rape (Street et al., 2009). At the other end of the spectrum of violence is sexual harassment and a hostile work environment. Sexual harassment includes coerced sexual involvement that is a condition of employment or used as the basis of employment-related decisions, such as assignment to a more desirable duty location or avoiding a poor performance appraisal (Street et al., 2009). It also includes any sexual behaviors that create an offensive, hostile, or intimidating work environment, such as making frequent unwanted sexual advances or making repeated offensive comments about a person's sexual activities (Street et al., 2009).

Over half of military women (52%) reported experiencing either offensive sexual behaviors, such as repeatedly being told offensive sexual stories or jokes, or experiencing unwelcome attempts at being drawn into discussions of sexual matters (Street et al., 2009). When screened by Department of Veterans Affairs medical practitioners in 2010, 0.7% of men and 15.1% of women veterans of Operation Iraqi Freedom/Operation Enduring Freedom reported experiencing military sexual trauma (Mattocks et al., 2012). Studies have shown that MST plays a more significant role in explaining PTSD than does combat exposure or other wartime stressor (Carlson, Stromwall, & Lietz, 2013).

Interpersonal Stressors.   Women veterans may experience additional "psychosocial stressors" different from their male colleagues (Gunter-Hunt et al., 2013, p. 28). These stressors can include separation from spouses and children, and poor social support from family (Gunter-Hunt et al., 2013; Street et al., 2009). Women veterans are also more likely to have experienced gender harassment, behaviors that are not sexually based but are hostile or degrading and occur based on one's biological sex (Street et al., 2009). These behaviors become apparent when one gender attempts to reinforce traditional gender roles or expects one gender to work harder than the other to prove capability or the ability to assimilate. Scholars believe that gender harassment occurs more frequently than other forms of sexual harassment, with recent data indicating that 54% of women service members experience some form of gender harassment each year (Street et al., 2009).

Homecoming Adjustment.   Understanding that the family is a critical source of support for the service member, it is important to consider the impact of the military member's separation from and reintegration into the family unit as an outcome of deployment (Street et al., 2009). The impact of deployment on men and women serving in the military may be different as a result of women's traditional responsibilities at home (Mattocks et al., 2012). Although the gap in household responsibilities has narrowed over the years, women report still having more responsibilities for childcare, parent care, housekeeping, and cooking meals (Mattocks et al., 2012). Thus, when the women service member deploys, leaving the family at home, additional stress occurs. Studies highlight that over 40% of military women have children and that the rising divorce rates for military women places an added stress on women who must find alternate arrangements for childcare and family welfare during their deployment (DiRamio et al., 2015; Mattocks et al., 2012; Street et al., 2009).

Women Warriors as Veterans

Another factor that may affect the woman service member's homecoming adjustment is coping with her newfound "woman veteran" identity:

> While our society has made great strides towards the acceptance of women as Veterans over recent decades, some sectors of society may not yet comfortably embrace this concept and some women's homecoming may, therefore, be impacted by the perception that women are not "real Veterans" or that they are not exposed to "real danger" relative to Veteran men. (Street et al., 2009, p. 692)

Not having full acceptance of their veteran identity may cause women veterans additional stress during reentry into civilian life.

Women veterans also report feeling even more isolated as peer support and networking opportunities with other women are lacking during and after deployments (Demers, 2013; Foster & Vince, 2009). As these women veterans reenter the civilian world, many will feel invisible to society as they navigate through their transition process and come to terms with their new civilian life and its associated challenges (Foster & Vince, 2009; Santovec, 2012).

A 2009 Department of Veterans Affairs study (National Center for Veterans Analysis and Statistics [NCVAS], 2011) found that women comprised only 9% of the total veteran population in the United States (1.5 million women), but projected that by 2035 they will make up over 15% of veterans. This same study highlighted that 71% of women veterans served in time of war, with almost half of them (735,000) serving during the Gulf War era (August 1990 to the present), with most being eligible for GI Bill educational benefits.

NEW DIRECTIONS FOR COMMUNITY COLLEGES • DOI: 10.1002/cc

The latest published enrollment statistics from the Department of Veterans Affairs show 284,000 women veterans (19% of all women veterans) used their GI Bill benefits to fund all or part of their college education for undergraduate or community college purposes (NCVAS, 2011). As seen in California, that usage is expected to grow, as community colleges in the state enroll over 44,000 veterans (California Community College Chancellor's Office, 2016). The sustained usage of the GI Bill college benefits will continue to have an impact on community colleges across the country, requiring that they take measures to facilitate the academic success of and, ultimately, enable the women–veterans' successful transition to civilian life (Baechtold & De Sawal, 2009; DiRamio & Jarvis, 2011).

Women veterans "bring assets and strengths to campus and to their individual lives," and it is essential that college leaders "broaden the paradigm of the student–veteran from deficits to strengths, from shortcomings to possibilities, and from isolation to community" (Iverson & Anderson, 2013, p. 106). Instead of viewing women veterans from a deficit perspective, it is critical to find supports for these individuals as they make the transition from the military back home and, specifically, into the nation's community colleges. Supporting and acknowledging this group can have a positive impact on the entire campus.

Women Veterans as Community College Students

I recently conducted a qualitative study (Heineman, 2016) that investigated the transition experiences of women student–veterans who enrolled in the community college after completing their military active duty service. As part of this study, I conducted 19 individual, semistructured interviews with women student–veterans attending two large, suburban southern California community colleges, each enrolling over 17,000 students annually. Using a constructivist, grounded theory methodology, I created a model consisting of four related themes showing how women veterans were managing their transition into the role of community college student. The themes included (a) a gendered military experience; (b) finding her way; (c) preparing for change; and (d) relying on support, which resulted in the creation of a transition model for women veterans.

The central component of the model was "Finding Her Way," with its three associated subthemes influencing this element. Each of the elements exerted mutual influence on one another. Leaving active duty military service and becoming a civilian college student was an evolutionary process for the participants. Each woman charted her own path as a student-veteran, and most seemed content with their college-student status, having left their military lives behind them. Izzie[1], a 29-year-old Navy veteran, explained: "You get to be you again. Whereas in the Navy … it's about the Navy, and that's what you're there for. You're there to do a job and get through." All the participants were coming to terms with their newfound independence from military rules and their veteran identities. Finally, most participants appeared willing to seek help for academic challenges but were hesitant to seek social interactions with peers on campus.

Although "Finding Her Way" was the central component of the model, "a gendered military experience" was the most influential force on how participants were transitioning to their new role of student–veterans. The military experience of participants (i.e., their feelings of marginalization and alienation) appeared to have negatively influenced their desire to socialize on campus. When study participants became pregnant on active duty, they were reassigned to less desirable (or less promotable) jobs—off ship or in from the field—as required by military regulations to protect the mother and child. "As soon as you realized you were pregnant you had to leave the ship," explained Donna, a 26-year-old Navy veteran. Physical injuries also contributed to a feeling of marginalization. Despite seeking medical attention for hip stress fractures incurred while in the Marine Corps, Nancy felt devalued as a Marine, especially after talking to one healthcare provider: "I got to hear him talking about how females fake their injuries, because they don't wanna work out, or because they want to get out or—those sorts of things."

Their hesitation to socialize with male student–veteran peers further complicated their ability to "fit in" on campus. Having felt rejected by and alienated from their male peers when on active duty, the participants preferred to avoid possible similar encounters in the veterans resource centers (VRC) and on campus. This reluctance could explain the limited number of study participants who were familiar with or who routinely visited the campus' VRCs. Their hesitation to socialize may be contributing to the participants' desire to hide their veteran identity on campus in an effort to avoid remembering negative active duty experiences.

Their gendered military experience also influenced the model component of "relying on support." Participants knew that they could rely on family as they became college students. These same family members supported them in their other life-changing decisions: joining and leaving the military service. Throughout their military experience, the participants learned that they could rely on others for direction, guidance, and advice, especially if this reliance was on someone considered an authority figure (someone older, more senior or mature). The participants willingly sought out and accepted help from college faculty and staff (i.e., authority figures). Gloria, a 30-year-old Navy veteran, was most impressed with faculty availability and their willingness to engage with students: "When I went to college 12 years ago, I just don't remember instructors emailing us, 'We are here. Do you have questions? We're paid to answer your questions'... and they're very just welcoming. It's nice."

There was a mutual influence between the model components of relying on support and preparing for change in their lives. As with their decisions to join and leave military service, most participants consulted with family and close (nonmilitary) friends in their decision to enroll at the community college.[2] Advice from this support network helped participants prepare themselves financially for life after active duty. Knowing where to go for assistance was a skill learned while on active duty. Participants willingly relied on college faculty and staff to assist with academic challenges or with their post-9/11 GI Bill benefits.

I found that women student–veterans were focused, independent, and more mature than traditional community college students due to their unique, military experience. Because of their gendered military experience, however, they relied on a more individualized and self-focused approach to find their individual voices and personal identities as they transitioned to student–veteran status. As they come to terms with their student–veteran identity, the strongest influence on their ability or inability to "fit in" with the student population was their gendered military experiences, self-sufficiency, and life experiences. Evidence of this tendency was their limited classroom and campus encounters with fellow students and their apparent, self-imposed isolation. This isolation from peers is in stark contrast to their willingness to seek and accept help from college faculty and staff.

Overall, the study explained how women student–veterans were transitioning into their new roles as student–veterans. This research posits that these women will experience difficulties fitting in with the student population, and they will, selectively and discriminately, seek and accept help, preferring to retain their independence and will only occasionally self-identify as veterans. Their social interactions with male, military peers will be minimal, as will be their interactions with younger classmates. They will seek academic help when they need it, and they will rely on college faculty and staff for this support. The following section addresses accommodations colleges can make to increase support for these women student–veterans on their campuses.

Implications for Practice and Policy

Armed with information on how women veterans are managing their transition to community college students, community college leaders can more effectively support the social integration and educational success of women student–veterans. Understanding that "one size" does not "fit all" for women student–veterans, the following recommendations can stimulate review and improvement of existing college programs, practices, and policies.

Recognizing that several colleges are already offering some of these services, these recommendations can encourage colleges to continue delivering them. This listing also serves as a motivator for those colleges that have yet to provide these services and to highlight the additional measures they can take to enhance the success of this underserved, and perhaps invisible, student population.

NEW DIRECTIONS FOR COMMUNITY COLLEGES • DOI: 10.1002/cc

Provide Supportive Academic Resources. Women student–veterans may experience initial, but minimal, academic challenges as they return to the classroom. Many of the women veterans were last exposed to basic mathematics and writing concepts in high school and may find that they need additional support in relearning these fundamental and foundational skills. Because of their poor performance on the college's placement tests, many of the participants in the study placed into remedial or basic mathematics classes. An intervention might include community colleges offering mathematics "boot camps" to provide a review of basic concepts in advance of the placement tests and understanding that it was many years since these women engaged in higher mathematics. This boot camp experience can enable women student–veterans to perform better on the required placement tests, allowing them to enroll in more advanced classes, which can provide a faster track to completion. Community college leaders must continue to provide essential academic resources (i.e., tutoring, mathematics, and writing clinics) for women student–veterans to enable their continued success.

Provide Sensitivity Training for Faculty and Staff on Women Student–Veteran Issues. Women student–veterans will solicit support from those they trust to receive needed academic or support help. In the community college environment, the women will work closely with their classroom faculty, Veterans Affairs certifying officials, and counselors. Knowing that they are critical points of support, faculty members and staff need awareness about the challenges women student–veterans faced while on active duty (i.e., their gendered military experience, PTSD, and/or MST). Sensitivity training for faculty and staff who work with women student–veterans in various campus offices or in the classroom could address and alleviate many of the issues facing these students.

Provide a College Orientation for New Faculty and Staff. As new faculty and staff begin their own community college experience, many may not be familiar with the student support resources on their campus. This unfamiliarity with available resources (e.g., tutoring services, mental health counseling, financial services) could result in missed opportunities to support the women student–veterans who will be coming to them for assistance. Providing periodic resource awareness training can empower faculty and staff to recommend these services to their students. This awareness can also inspire and motivate faculty members to include this resource information in their syllabi, further advertising campus support services to all students.

Develop Women Student–Veteran Workshops and Create a Welcoming VRC Environment. Women student–veterans may feel isolated on campus. They may not fit in socially with younger students, as the veterans are likely older and more mature. They may correspondingly desire to distance themselves from male student–veteran peers on campus in an effort to prevent negative military memories from resurfacing. Community college leaders can promote interactions among women student–veterans by helping them self-identify among their peers and by creating social opportunities solely for women student–veterans. Workshops for women student–veterans can help promote time to interact with others and can include topics such as stress reduction and anger management techniques, financial literacy, legal affairs, and methods for fine-tuning interpersonal and communication skills.

The majority of study participants were unaware of the VRC and were not using the center's services (e.g., computers, printers, social opportunities, peer-tutoring services). Through enhanced advertising and creating "meet-and-greet" opportunities for women student–veterans, the VRC could become more accessible to women student–veterans. However, if the women do not feel comfortable engaging in the VRC, it will be unlikely that they will use its services, regardless of the value the services provide. It is incumbent on the community college leadership to look at the VRC environment and ensure that it is welcoming to all student–veterans. This welcoming environment could include posting of pictures, prints, or photos of women military members in addition to the traditional masculine displays of military power.

Provide Childcare Services for Women Student–Veterans.   Because women student–veterans are likely older than the typical community college student, they may be dealing with childcare concerns. Challenges with childcare surfaced during my study as a key reason for the departure of my participants from active duty service. Having been separated from their children frequently while on active duty (i.e., war zone deployments and/or sea duty), women veterans may desire to provide additional support to their children to "make up for lost time." To keep these women enrolled at the community college, addressing childcare issues becomes crucial. Ensuring academic support, while simultaneously addressing childcare concerns, is important for the success of women student–veterans. For example, any college-sponsored social or academic opportunities for these students should promote or expand current childcare services to garner active attendance and participation.

Establish a Women Student–Veteran Mentoring Program With Community Partners.   Familiar with the concept of mentoring from their military experience, most women veterans would understand the value of and appreciate the collegial support of a focused mentoring program. Assigning the women student–veterans mentors in the local community who have ties to higher education or their desired career paths can provide a strong support structure and connections to job opportunities. For example, women student–veterans could be partnered with women leaders at the local branches of the American Association of University Women (AAUW). In addition to facilitating the transition to the college environment, this mentoring relationship could encourage enrollment in science, technology, engineering, and mathematics (STEM) fields that have traditionally seen underrepresentation by women in college and in industry. Mentoring

NEW DIRECTIONS FOR COMMUNITY COLLEGES • DOI: 10.1002/cc

opportunities between women student–veterans and members of the local chamber of commerce provide another opportunity for networking. The students would learn about business leadership challenges, which may parallel challenges they faced and overcame in their military experience. These mentoring relationships would also enhance their social skills through business networking opportunities. Finally, these partnerships could open future employment opportunities for the students once they finish their degrees.

Conclusion

Community college leaders, faculty, and staff should recognize the strength, independence, and resiliency that women student–veterans bring into the classroom. This essential recognition of ability can shift the focus from viewing the women student–veterans from a deficit base and instead shift the perspective to an asset-based orientation. Campus leaders can better understand the experiences of women student–veterans when they recognize how the women's past military experiences contributes to their sense of self. Because women veterans have had a gendered experience during their military service, they are reluctant to associate with male veterans and as a result often miss connecting with critical support services on campus. Knowing whom women student–veterans rely on for support (authority figures) and how they rely on their family and friends for support can provide key advocates for the women during their time at the community college. Community colleges, in appropriately welcoming these students, will benefit the college, the local community, and the veteran—delivering a positive outcome for all involved.

Note

1. Pseudonyms were used for all study participants.
2. Although they attended federally mandated transition assistance classes prior to separating from the military, most found the information provided in these classes to be too basic and not timely.

References

American Association of Community Colleges. (2016). *2016 fact sheet*. Retrieved from http://www.aacc.nche.edu/AboutCC/Documents/AACCFactSheetsR2.pdf
Baechtold, M., & De Sawal, D. M. (2009). Meeting the needs of women veterans. In R. Ackerman & D. DiRamio (Eds.), *New Directions for Student Services: No. 126. Creating a veteran-friendly campus: Strategies for transition success* (pp. 35–43). San Francisco, CA: Jossey-Bass. https://doi.org/10.1002/ss.314
California Community College Chancellor's Office. (2016). *Veterans services* [Press release]. Retrieved from http://extranet.cccco.edu/Portals/1/SSSP/AboutSSSP/Programs/Fact Sheet Veterans 5-14.pdf

Carlson, B. E., Stromwall, L. K., & Lietz, C. A. (2013). Mental health issues in recently returning women veterans: Implications for practice. *Social Work*, 58(2), 105–114.

Demers, A. L. (2013). From death to life: Female veterans, identity negotiation, and reintegration into society. *Journal of Humanistic Psychology*, 53(4), 489–515. https://doi.org/10.1177/0022167812472395

DiRamio, D., & Jarvis, K. (2011). Special issue: Veterans in higher education—When Johnny and Jane come marching to campus. [*ASHE Higher Education Report*, 37(3)]. San Francisco, CA: Jossey-Bass. https://doi.org/10.1002/aehe.3703

DiRamio, D., Jarvis, K., Iverson, S., Seher, C., & Anderson, R. (2015). Out from the shadows: Female student veterans and help-seeking. *College Student Journal*, 49(1), 49–68.

Foster, L. K., & Vince, S. (2009). *California's women veterans: Challenges and needs of those who served* (CRB 09-009). Sacramento: California Research Bureau.

Gunter-Hunt, G., Feldman, J., Gendron, J., Bonney, A., & Unger, J. (2013). Outreach to women veterans of Iraq and Afghanistan: A VA and national guard collaboration. *Federal Practitioner*, 30(2), 25–46.

Hamrick, F., & Rumann, C. (2012). Addressing the needs of women servicemembers and veterans in higher education. *On Campus with Women*, 40(3), 1–5.

Heineman, J. A. (2016). *From boots to suits: Women veterans transitioning to community college students* (Doctoral dissertation). San Diego State University, San Diego, CA.

Iverson, S., & Anderson, R. (2013). The complexity of veteran identity. Understanding the role of gender, race, and sexuality. In F. Hamrick & C. Rumann (Eds.), *Called to serve. A handbook on student veterans and higher education* (pp. 89–113). San Francisco, CA: Jossey-Bass.

Lighthall, A. (2012). Ten things you should know about today's student veteran. *Thought & Action*, 28, 81–90.

Mattocks, K. M., Haskell, S. G., Krebs, E. E., Justice, A. C., Yano, E. M., & Brandt, C. (2012). Women at war: Understanding how women veterans cope with combat and military sexual trauma. *Social Science and Medicine*, 74(4), 537–545.

McBain, L., Kim, Y., Cook, B., & Snead, K. (2012). *From soldier to student II: Assessing campus programs for veterans and service members*. Retrieved from http://www.acenet.edu/news-room/Pages/From-Soldier-to-Student-II.aspx

Murdoch, M., Bradley, A., Mather, S. H., Klein, R. E., Turner, C. L., & Yano, E. M. (2006). Women and war. *Journal of General Internal Medicine*, 21(S3), S5–S10.

National Center for Veterans Analysis and Statistics. (2011). *America's women veterans: Military service history and VA benefit utilization statistics*. Washington, DC: U.S. Department of Veterans Affairs.

O'Herrin, E. (2011). Enhancing veteran success in higher education. *Peer Review*, 13(1), 15–18.

Persky, K. R., & Oliver, D. E. (2010). Veterans coming home to the community college: Linking research to practice. *Community College Journal of Research and Practice*, 35 (1–2), 111–120. https://doi.org/10.1080/10668926.2011.525184

Radford, A. W. (2011). *Military service members and veterans: A profile of those enrolled in undergraduate and graduate education in 2007–2008* (NCES 2011-163). Washington, DC: National Center for Education Statistics. Retrieved from https://nces.ed.gov/pubsearch/pubsinfo.asp?pubid=2011163

Rumann, C., & Hamrick, F. (2010). Student veterans in transition: Re-enrolling after war zone deployments. *Journal of Higher Education*, 81(4), 431–458.

Rumann, C., Rivera, M., & Hernandez, I. (2011). Student veterans and community colleges. In E. M. Cox & J. S. Watson (Eds.), *New Directions for Community Colleges: No. 155. Marginalized students* (pp. 51–58). San Francisco, CA: Jossey-Bass. https://doi.org/10.1002/cc.457

Santovec, M. L. (2012). Women veterans: "Invisible warriors" on your campus. *Women in Higher Education, 21*(11), 21–22.

Street, A. E., Vogt, D., & Dutra, L. (2009). A new generation of women veterans: Stressors faced by women deployed to Iraq and Afghanistan. *Clinical Psychology Review, 29*(8), 685–694.

U.S. Department of Veterans Affairs. (2010). *Review of combat stress in women veterans receiving VA health care and disability benefits.* Washington, DC: Author. Retrieved from http://www.va.gov/oig/52/reports/2011/VAOIG-10-01640-45.pdf

Wheeler, H. A. (2012). Veterans' transitions to community college: A case study. *Community College Journal of Research and Practice, 36*(10), 775–792.

Judie Heineman, a retired U.S. Navy captain, served on active duty in the Navy for almost 28 years. She earned her doctorate in education from San Diego State University.

8

This chapter explores the role of gender as a critical aspect of identity formation. The chapter reviews how narrow definitions of gender deeply shape campus climate, particularly for individuals who challenge norms in terms of gender identity, gender expression, and gender roles.

Conflating Gender and Identity: The Need for Gender-Fluid Programming in Community Colleges

Eboni M. Zamani-Gallaher

Higher education institutions as microcosms of larger society are experiencing a changing face. According to the U.S. Department of Education (2015), changes in college attendance by race and ethnicity in college enrollment rates for 1990 in contrast to 2014 were as follows: Whites—44% versus 35%; Blacks—25% versus 37%; and Hispanics—16% versus 39%. Coupled with demographic shifts by race/ethnicity, the gender composition of post-secondary attendees has changed over the last 25 years.

In 1990, 6 in 10 graduating female high school students enrolled in college without any lag time. At present, nearly three fourths of female high school completers (i.e., 73%) immediately enroll in college compared to 64% of males at 2- and 4-year colleges (Kena et al., 2016). The rate for male high school completers in 2014 has remained roughly the same as it was in 1990. Women currently represent 57% of college attendees, a rate that has been stable since 2003 (U.S. Department of Education, 2016a). These data underscore that a higher percentage of women collegians participate in higher education in contrast to the number of females in the general population.

Gender and Student Diversity

When looking closely at 2-year college enrollment by gender, similar trends emerge, but differences exist when looking at race/ethnicity. Among all undergraduates, 62% of American Indian, 57% of Hispanic, 52% of Black,

New Directions for Community Colleges, no. 179, Fall 2017 © 2017 Wiley Periodicals, Inc.
Published online in Wiley Online Library (wileyonlinelibrary.com) • DOI: 10.1002/cc.20265

and 43% of Asian American/Pacific Islander students enrolled in college are attending community colleges (American Association of Community Colleges, 2016). Trend data in community colleges illustrate an increasing number of White men (36% versus 40%) and Hispanic men (15% versus 30%) enrolled between 1990 and 2014. However, Black males were the exception as their college enrollment rate between 1990 and 2014 remained fairly stagnant (26% versus 28%).

What contributes to students enrolling in the community college? A class and racialized reality intersect for students that affect their choices, shape their experiences, affect their student outcomes, and subsequent career trajectories. However, this complexity is not commonly underscored or dissected in relation to student demographics and the ways they are intertwined. When considering racially/ethnically diverse students by gender, it is not only important that they enter higher education, but it is critical where they enter and who enters. For instance, do differences of opportunity exist when disaggregating women's enrollment alongside other student background characteristics to create equity gaps? As female and male identity is not monolithic, when we refer to women in higher education, who is included? How is *She* identified and designated? Who makes the determination of female? Furthermore, how does the binary of gender representation limit understanding of gender for faculty and administrative staff? Constructions of gender permeate the community college and affect students, faculty, and staff.

Gender and Faculty Diversity

When examining faculty by race, ethnicity, and gender at 2- and 4-year colleges, across rank, including full- and part-time status, in fall 2013, Whites comprised 78% of the 1.5 million faculty at degree-granting institutions (43% males, 35% females), 6% were Black faculty (3% males, 3% females), and Hispanics made up 4% of faculty (2% males, 2% females). Ten percent of faculty was Asian/Pacific Islander (6% males, 4% females) and less than 1% was American Indian/Alaska Native and of two or more races (U.S. Department of Education, 2016b).

Differences emerge in higher faculty ranks. Of full-time professors at full rank only, the majority are White males (58%), followed by White females (26%), 2% of full-time faculty were Black males, 1% Black females, 2% Hispanic males, 1% Hispanic females, 7% Asian/Pacific Islander males, and 2% Asian/Pacific Islander females (U.S. Department of Education, 2016b). There is noticeable stratification of the faculty relative to full-time status as well as rank by race, ethnicity, and gender. Like overall faculty representation, 80% of full-time community college faculty is White, but more women are faculty members at the community college (about 50%) compared to overall faculty members in 2- and 4-year colleges (44%; Cohen, Brawer, & Kisker, 2014). What is not evident in these figures is how the faculty members identify their gender or how gender intersects with race/ethnicity (e.g., transgender persons of color).

Constructing Gender: Identity and Expression

The aforementioned statistics skew information on race/ethnicity and gender as they do not adequately reflect how individuals have socially constructed their race and gender. Differences exist as race and gender are their social construction based on expected behaviors, abilities, roles, and interests. Self-defined identity is important to many minoritized, marginalized groups in terms of establishing their collective identity on their own terms. There are students and faculty members who do not ascribe to male or female gender categorizations nor do they care to be grouped with men or women. Problematic is the lack of data that accurately align with an individual's self-definition relative to gender identity in particular. Gender identities reflect how individuals conceive and conceptualize gender on their own terms versus ascribing to normalized social constructions of male and female. Gender as traditionally employed does not move beyond a referent point for one's biological sex. Thus, the traditional view of gender does not accommodate gender nonconformity or acknowledge gender fluidity but instead strictly adheres to male/female as the norm.

As gender denotes a socially constructed concept, gender identity comprises a spectrum of how individuals identify that is multidimensional and not linear, but rather a continuum of maleness, femaleness, and gender identities not bounded by the twofold of male or female. In many ways, gender identity is boundless whereas the term gender alone can be confining and restrictive and fuel gender bias. The socialization of gender relative to rules and roles are both implicit and explicit in educational norms and practices (e.g., the curriculum, faculty–student interactions, skewed participation by discipline/field of study, stratification of faculty and staff by gender, etc.). Hence, gender socialization experiences considered normative can present chilly campus climates for those who do not conform to conventional gender designations or traditional gender roles.

Beyond Nomenclature: Gender, Labels, and Mattering

> It is time that we all see gender as a spectrum instead of two sets of opposing ideals.
>
> Actress Emma Watson (United Nations Speech, September 20, 2014)

What is in a name? Naming has great importance as it specifies what something suggests, what may be desired, and who actually decides on what to give name to and how it will be referenced. Therefore, how gender is named has been traditionally normed by the sexual assignment at birth as opposed to what is organic to individuals in terms of gender being male, female, or identifying with neither or both. The naming of gender, the label assigned by gender to individuals matters as this extends gender identity, and how femininity and masculinity manifests or is expressed. As such, our innate sense of being male or female is reflective of gender identity and gender expression. According to Killermann (2013), gender is expressed daily in how we carry ourselves, dress, wear our hair, talk, and move among others, as these behaviors signal how we see ourselves and the extent to which that may or may not align with societal expectations of being male or female. There arguably is a fluidity of gender with regard to femininity and masculinity, as some do not conform to normative ideas of maleness and femaleness to govern how they act, behave, or think per the male or female sex assigned at birth.

Transgender and genderqueer (i.e., gender nonconforming) persons who have a sense of agency to be themselves face gender-role conflict in terms of negative consequences. Some examples include facing danger and enduring unpleasant conditions for being true to their self-concept, gender expression, and identity that does not abide with the binary conceptualization of male/female or gender norms associated with their sex. Those identifying with gender-normed constructions of female or male do not face these challenges.

Cisprivilege

The conflation of gender expression and gender identity excludes sexuality. Those who are gender nonconforming cut across many cultural groups and represent diversity by race, ethnicity, nationality, age, sex, religious background, disability, and social class (Killermann, 2013). The degree to which one identifies with gender norms (except sexual orientation), as well as with the sex assigned at birth, is indicative of being a cisgender person. Cisgender people accrue privilege by virtue of having alignment with normalized notions of gender identity and the concept of cisprivilege acknowledges the benefits resulting from cisgender identity. Akin to male privilege and White privilege, cisprivilege affords preferential treatment and opportunities to those who identify inside the male/female gender binary. Cisprivilege manifests in not being concerned about behaving in a way that is considered incorrect by gender norms/roles; not having to be referred to by the wrong gender pronoun, worry about public facilities (e.g., restrooms, department store changing rooms, gym locker rooms, etc.) accommodating you, or being treated differently for your gender expression/identity (Killermann, 2013; Nicolazzo, 2016).

Individuals identifying as heterosexual, as well as White gay and bisexual men who bear gender expression and gender identities that align with socially constructed norms, benefit from cisprivilege because Whiteness and being male afford advantages or rights solely on the basis of their race and sex. Although men have access to male privilege, the extent of that privilege can vary and is dependent on characteristics such as race, social class, sexual orientation, disability, etc. Hence, among minoritized gender groups and sexualities, White lesbian or bisexual women benefit from White privilege, though there are limited advantages or rights made available to them due to male dominated gender norms and heterosexism. The term cisgender privilege is referenced in lesbian, gay, bisexual, transgender, and queer (LGBTQ) literature; however, there is little mention or study of postsecondary education institutions that actively seek to curb cisprivilege and promote inclusion of gender nonconforming/transgender individuals by having nondiscrimination policies that incorporate gender expression and identity. According to Campus Pride (2016), 998 colleges and universities include gender expression and gender identity in their institutional nondiscrimination policy statements, with 212 associate degree granting institutions among this listing (see https://www.campuspride.org/tpc/nondiscrimination/).

There are 260 postsecondary education institutions categorized as LGBTQ-friendly campuses according to the Campus Pride Index. Only 18 out of the 260 LGBTQ-Friendly Campuses in the Campus Pride Index are community colleges. Eight of the 18 LGBTQ-Friendly Community College Campuses in the Campus Pride Index also have explicit nondiscrimination policies that include gender expression and gender identity.

The Campus Pride LGBTQ-Friendly Index emerged to provide a campus assessment of LGBTQ-friendly practices and policies. For 15 years, the index has provided educators with tools to improve LGBTQ campus life at their respective institutions and has been the benchmark for evaluating on a five-star rating system various LGBTQ-friendly factors such as policies, programming, and practices responsive to sexual orientation, gender identity/expression and other areas of inclusion. Of note, there are no community colleges among the top 30 LGBTQ-friendly campuses scoring the highest percentages for policies, programs, and practices.

The College Equality Index (CEI) is another tool that seeks to provide information on inclusive LGBTQ campus environments, in particular trans-friendly campuses highlighting institutions that offer domestic partner benefits and have sexual orientation and gender identity nondiscrimination statements, gender neutral restrooms, and housing (here again, no community colleges are noted). Per the U.S. Department of Education (n.d.) guidelines, colleges and universities that do not include gender identity or state gender expression in their nondiscrimination policies are required under Title IX to forbid transgender student discrimination.

Gender relative to sexual assignment, expression, and identity demonstrate intersecting selves and the complexity of socially constructed notions of self in contrast to self-definitions of personhood. The complications and shortcomings of institutions observing identities outside of dominant ideologies and mainstream culture are evident in the prejudice, discrimination, and chilly climates many LGBTQ, intersex, asexual, and gender-nonconforming persons face on college campuses.

Gender Construction and the Community College Context

There are diverse meanings attached to gender in terms of who frames it, how assumptions about gender neutrality remain unexamined, and whether gender equality is achievable. There is a dearth of literature that examines gender beyond the dichotomy of male or female and that teases out how students reconcile self and define identity across multiple group membership by race/ethnicity, class, sexuality, ability, religion, nationality, etc. (Zamani-Gallaher & Choudhuri, 2016). Gender sits at the contested and contextual cross-section of the microcultural multiplicity of selves (Hobson, 2003). Of the literature that pays sufficient attention to gender in higher education, in particular gender discrimination, gender identity, gender expression and/or gender roles, the perspectives of students, faculty, and staff within 4-year contexts are primary and focus on community college students or educators is slight (Harris & Harper, 2008; Zamani-Gallaher & Choudhuri, 2016). This gap in research underscores the importance of this volume dedicated to gender in community college contexts.

Research on gender in community colleges settings has explored the narrow definitions of gender, the formation of gender roles, images of gender, segmentation of opportunity by gender, devaluing of individuals by gender, and gender performance in community college settings (Eddy & Cox, 2008; Harris & Harper, 2008; Lester, 2008, 2011; Townsend & Twombly, 2007a, 2007b; VanDerLinden, 2004). How people construct their identities is reflective of their experiences. Identity development is not static in nature but influenced by other background characteristics such as class and race that can often be neglected (Tett, 2000). Scant research exists on the nuances of gender identity in the community college context.

Applying feminist phase theory, Twombly (1993) conducted an exhaustive study that examined the consideration of women in community college literature. At the time, little focus on women in administrative and faculty roles occurred despite two out of five community college faculty being women. Twombly (1993) asserted that not only were there few articles focused on women, but those that existed at the time did not treat gender, race, ethnicity, or class in a comprehensive manner (e.g., traditionally feminist scholars focused primarily on White middle-class women). Twombly suggested that a lag in the community college literature to reflect attention to issues of race, ethnicity, and class resulted in part to the absence of scholars of color represented among those writing and concluded that failing to examine the relationship of race, class, and gender in community colleges is inexcusable. Some progress has occurred over the past 25 years since Twombly first highlighted these issues, but much work remains.

NEW DIRECTIONS FOR COMMUNITY COLLEGES • DOI: 10.1002/cc

Community College Campus Climate. The 2-year college sector is known for promoting access and broadening participation, yet support for the concerns of women, people of color, LGBTQ individuals, and other minoritized groups relative to community college research is wanting (Amey, VanDerLinden, & Brown, 2002; Twombly, 1993; Zamani-Gallaher & Choudhuri, 2011, 2016). Adapting the institutional climate for diversity framework by Hurtado, Milem, Clayton-Pederson, and Allen (1999) for assessing the climate for community college faculty using National Center for Education Statistics (NCES) community college data, Hagedorn and Laden (2002) found differences in the perceptions of campus climate with a slight gender effect of more women perceiving the climate as chilly. Overall, the findings demonstrated that women felt more discriminated against than men did, and women of color perceived greater discrimination than white women did. Similarly, Bonner (2001) asserted that there are differences in the experiences of female faculty of color in contrast to their White counterparts, with women of color on the faculty having the double jeopardy of facing racism and sexism across 2- and 4-year institutions, historically Black colleges and universities (HBCUs), and predominantly White institutions (PWIs). As a result, the way in which gender is operationalized is not necessarily inclusive of all (i.e., beyond the gender binary) nor the varying experiences within and between diverse groups by gender and race despite the institutional context. The politics of identity are germane yet are hidden in community colleges as the institutional context highlights access and equal opportunity. The open access mission of community colleges does not automatically exempt the institutions from inequities.

Other research on women in community colleges perspectives of campus climate for female faculty explored the experiences of those who were mothers. Wolf-Wendel, Ward, and Twombly (2007) examined the juggling act of balancing the faculty role with that of motherhood at 2-year colleges finding that community colleges present the life as an academic that does not mitigate the challenges of constraints on time, inequities at work, and balancing personal and professional demand but does appear to provide opportunities for greater work–life balance. However, the study was limited with participants being exclusively full-time female faculty in nontechnical areas who were mothers to young children. For more on this topic, see Ward and Wolf-Wendel's chapter in this volume.

Paradigm Shifts: Getting Beyond Confining Definitions of Identity. Over the last 5 years, the pendulum has swung relative to how colleges and universities frame gender, gender identity, gender expression, and sexual identity. For example, privately controlled Elmhurst College in Illinois became the first institution of higher education to include a question regarding LGBTQ identity on undergraduate applications for admissions in 2011 (Smith, 2012). Even though the question of LGBTQ identity did not influence admissions decisions, it was used to include qualifying students for a diversity scholarship. The next year Massachusetts Institute of Technology (MIT) began adding sexual orientation/gender identity on its admissions application, and in the same year the University of Iowa became the first public higher education institution to revise its admissions application to include sexual orientation, gender identity, and a transgender choice under gender questions (Jaschik, 2012).

Other institutions have since followed suit in an effort to signal a welcoming campus climate and to initiate a track record of attracting and graduating students that are gender nonconforming in terms of gender expression and identity and/or members of the LGBTQ community. In 2013, the Washington State Community and Technical College System (WSCTCS) began asking students questions about their sexual orientation and their gender identity on registration forms. The questions are optional and confidential, but the data collection will enable WSCTCS to become the first to employ a systemwide effort of 2-year colleges to collect data on LGBTQ students to track enrollment trends, retention, and success. This information can aid their faculty and staff in better serving the needs of LGBTQ students such as tailoring student support services and adding gender-neutral facilities (Ingeno, 2013).

Beyond the addition of questions on admissions applications or registration forms pertaining to sexual orientation and gender identity, some community colleges are seeking to be more responsive to gender expression, gender identity, and LGBTQ membership in terms of institutional policies. Even though Campus Pride has a list of institutions that include gender expression and gender identity in their policy statements, it is unclear how often updates occur or whether the list comprehensively reflects all of the 2-year institutions that have inclusive policy statements. Case in point, Ivy Tech Community College in Indiana has a transgender and gender-nonconforming nondiscrimination policy that expresses a desire to "ensure the safety, comfort, and healthy development of transgender or gender nonconforming students while maximizing integration and minimizing stigmatization of the individual" (n.d., p. 1). Yet, Ivy Tech is not among the community colleges on the Campus Pride list of institutions with nondiscrimination statements that include gender expression and gender identity. Ivy Tech Community College's policy ensures privacy for transgender students, as faculty/staff are to keep that information confidential, understanding that students exercise their right to discuss gender identity openly or keep it private. Additionally, Ivy Tech's policy clearly states procedures in the case of harassment or discrimination; the college position is that students have the right to dress consistent with their gender expression and identity, have the right to use facilities that correspond with their gender identity, and be addressed by their preferred name and pronoun that corresponds with their gender identity.

Conclusion

Granting that community colleges are considered more gender equitable than other institutional types (Townsend, 2008; Wolf-Wendel et al., 2007), there remains a continued need for community college policies, practices, programming, and research to do more in acknowledging and critiquing gender on campus. An intersectional approach to researching gender that employs theoretical frameworks such as feminist intersectional theory (Galupo et al., 2014) could aid in furthering our understanding of the diversity within diverse groups. The systems of privilege (i.e., cisgender privilege) operating against gender and sexual minoritized people often relegate individuals to having nonnormative identities that present a deficit. Even though there is literature that explores the experiences of women from a traditional perspective, a need exists for more diverse conceptualization of gender and the intersectionality of gender with other aspects of self for those at community college campuses.

References

American Association of Community College. (2016). *2016 fact sheet*. Retrieved from http://www.aacc.nche.edu/AboutCC/Documents/AACCFactSheetsR2.pdf

Amey, M. J., VanDerLinden, K. E., & Brown, D. F. (2002). Perspectives on community college leadership: Twenty years in the making. *Community College Journal of Research and Practice*, 26(7–8), 573–589.

Bonner, F. A. (2001). Addressing gender issues in the historically Black college and university community: A challenge and call to action. *Journal of Negro Education*, 70(3), 176–191.

Campus Pride. (2016). *Colleges and universities with nondiscrimination policies that include gender identity/expression*. Retrieved from https://www.campuspride.org/tpc/nondiscrimination/

Cohen, A. M., Brawer, F. B., & Kisker, C.B., (2014). *The American community college* (6th ed.). San Francisco, CA: Jossey-Bass.

Eddy, P. L., & Cox, E. M. (2008). Gendered leadership: An organizational perspective. In J. Lester (Ed.), *New Directions for Community Colleges: No. 142. Gendered perspectives on community colleges* (pp. 69–79). San Francisco, CA: Jossey-Bass.

Galupo, M. P., Bauerband, L. A., Gonzalez, K. A., Hagen, D. B., Hether, S. D., & Krum, T. E. (2014). Transgender friendship experiences: Benefits and barriers of friendships across gender identity and sexual orientation. *Feminism & Psychology*, 24(2), 193–215.

Hagedorn, L. S., & Laden, B. V. (2002). Exploring the climate for women as community college faculty. In C. L. Outcalt (Ed.), *New Directions for Community Colleges: No, 118. Community college faculty: Characteristics, practices, and challenges* (pp. 69–78). San Francisco, CA: Jossey-Bass.

Harris, F., & Harper, S. R. (2008). Masculinities go to community college: Understanding male identity socialization and gender role conflict. In J. Lester (Ed.), *New Directions for Community Colleges: No. 142. Gendered perspectives on community colleges* (pp. 25–35). San Francisco, CA: Jossey-Bass.

Hobson, B. (Ed.). (2003). *Recognition struggles and social movements: Contested identities, agency and power*. Cambridge, MA: Cambridge University Press.

Hurtado, S., Milem, J., Clayton-Pederson, A., & Allen, W. (1999). Enacting diverse learning environments: Improving the climate for racial/ethnic diversity in higher education. [ASHE-ERIC Higher Education Reports, 26(8)]. San Francisco, CA: Jossey-Bass.

Ingeno, L. (2013, August 5). Ask, do tell: Washington State's community colleges femininity voluntary questions about sexual orientation and gender identity to all student registration forms. Inside Higher Education. Retrieved from https://www.insidehighered.com/news/2013/08/05/washington-state-2-year-colleges-will-ask-students-about-sexual-orientation

Ivy Tech Community College. (n.d.). Transgender policy. Retrieved from https://www.ivytech.edu/files/9.3.1-Transgender-Policy.pdf

Jaschik, S. (2012, December 12). U. of Iowa will ask: Applicants don't have to tell, but they can indicate their identification as gay, and can select transgender as their gender. Inside Higher Education. Retrieved from https://www.insidehighered.com/news/2012/12/12/university-iowa-adds-optional-question-sexual-orientation

Kena, G., Hussar, W., McFarland, J., de Brey, C., Musu-Gillette, L., Wang, X., ... Dunlop Velez, E. (2016, May 26). The condition of education 2016. Washington, DC: U.S. Department of Education, National Center for Education Statistics.

Killermann, S. (2013). The social justice advocate's handbook: A guide to gender. Austin, TX: Impetus Books.

Lester, J. (2008). Performing gender in the workplace gender socialization, power, and identity among women faculty members. Community College Review, 35(4), 277–305.

Lester, J. (2011). Regulating gender performances: Power and gender norms in faculty work. NASPA Journal about Women in Higher Education, 4(2), 142–169.

Nicolazzo, Z. (2016). Trans* in college: Transgender students' strategies for navigating campus life and the institutional politics of inclusion. Sterling, VA: Stylus.

Smith, M. (2012, January 16). No identity crisis: At Elmhurst College, most applicants are answering an optional question about sexual orientation. Inside Higher Education. Retrieved from https://www.insidehighered.com/news/2012/01/16/elmhurst-finds-success-question-sexual-orientation

Tett, L. (2000). "I'm working class and proud of it"— Gendered experiences of nontraditional participants in higher education. Gender and Education, 12(2), 183–194.

Townsend, B. K. (2008). Community colleges as gender equitable institutions. In J. Lester (Ed.), New Directions for Community Colleges: No. 142. Gendered perspectives on community colleges (pp. 7–14). San Francisco, CA: Jossey-Bass.

Townsend, B. K., & Twombly, S. B. (2007a). Community college faculty: Overlooked and undervalued. [ASHE Higher Education Report, 32(6)]. San Francisco, CA: Jossey-Bass.

Townsend, B. K., & Twombly, S. B. (2007b). Accidental equity: The status of women in the community college. Equity & Excellence in Education, 40(3), 208–217.

Twombly, S. B. (1993). What we know about women in community colleges: An examination of the literature using feminist phase theory. Journal of Higher Education, 64(2), 186–210.

U.S. Department of Education, Office for Civil Rights. (n.d.). Questions and answers on Title IX and sexual violence. Retrieved from http://www2.ed.gov/about/offices/list/ocr/docs/qa-201404-title-ix.pdf

U.S. Department of Education, National Center for Education Statistics. (2015). Table 302.60: Enrollment rates of 18- to 24-year-olds in postsecondary degree-granting institutions, by sex and race/ethnicity: 1990 and 2014. In T. D. Snyder, C. de Brey, & S. A. Dillow, Digest of education statistics (51st ed.). Retrieved from http://nces.ed.gov/programs/coe/indicator_cpb.asp

U.S. Department of Education. (2016a). Digest of education statistics, 2014 (NCES 2016-006), Chapter 3. Washington, DC: National Center for Education Statistics. Retrieved from http://nces.ed.gov/fastfacts/display.asp?id=98

U.S. Department of Education, National Center for Education Statistics. (2016b). Table 315.20: Percentage distribution of full-time instructional faculty in degree-granting postsecondary institutions, by academic rank, selected race/ethnicity, and sex: Fall 2013. In G. Kena et al., *The condition of education 2016* (NCES 2016-144). Retrieved from https://nces.ed.gov/programs/coe/indicator_csc.asp

VanDerLinden, K. E. (2004). Gender differences in the preparation and promotion of community college administrators. *Community College Review, 31*(4), 1–24.

Watson, E. (2014, September 20). *Gender equality is your issue too.* Retrieved from http://www.unwomen.org/en/news/stories/2014/9/emma-watson-gender-equality-is-your-issue-too

Wolf-Wendel, L., Ward, K., & Twombly, S. B. (2007). Faculty life at community colleges: The perspective of women with children. *Community College Review, 34*(4), 255–281.

Zamani-Gallaher, E. M., & Choudhuri, D. D. (2011). A primer on LGBTQ students at community colleges: Considerations for research and practice. In E. M. Cox & J. S. Watson (Eds.), *New Directions for Community Colleges: No. 155., Marginalized students* (pp. 35–49). San Francisco, CA: Jossey-Bass.

Zamani-Gallaher, E. M., & Choudhuri, D. D. (2016). Tracing LGBTQ community college students' experiences. In C. C. Ozaki & R. L. Spaid (Eds.), *New Directions for Community Colleges: No. 174. Applying college change theories to student affairs practice* (pp. 47–63). San Francisco, CA: Jossey-Bass.

EBONI M. ZAMANI-GALLAHER *is a professor of higher education and director of the Office of Community College Research and Leadership at the University of Illinois-Champaign-Urbana. Her research focuses on community college students, student services, and equity.*

NEW DIRECTIONS FOR COMMUNITY COLLEGES • DOI: 10.1002/cc

9

This final chapter draws together the ways in which intersectionality occurs for a range of stakeholders regarding constructions of gender in community colleges and provides tactics for increasing equity.

Looking Forward—Strategies for Inclusivity

Pamela L. Eddy

In some respects, we can point to a number of ways in which women's advancement has occurred over the past 2 decades since Townsend's (1995) *New Directions for Community Colleges* (NDCC) on gender. Yes, there are more women in presidencies. Yes, faculty numbers represent parity between men and women in entry ranks. Yes, women have held steady in attendance at, and graduation from, community colleges. But inequities remain. Community colleges still lack leaders and faculty of color, despite enrolling the largest numbers of students of color (Snyder & Dillow, 2013). Narrow ideals of gender based on a binary are just starting to receive wider attention, and challenges exist in even the small advances made by trans* populations as witnessed by the legal battles in North Carolina regarding gender-neutral bathrooms (Blythe, 2016). So, yes, we've come a long way, but the road to equity remains long.

The pressing issues identified in the second NDCC volume dedicated to gender perspectives in community colleges included two main areas: affirmative action and expansion of gender construction (Eddy & Lester, 2008). In the decade since that publication, how gender is constructed is still central but has now moved beyond viewing gender construction based on subgroups, e.g., Black men, lesbian, gay, bisexual, transgender, queer (LGBTQ). Today, constructions of gender need to focus more on intersectionality (Cho, Crenshaw, & McCall, 2013). These topics and others are addressed in the following section, including the review of current gender issues in community colleges and suggestions for areas of future research. Finally, strategies are provided for various stakeholders to push for change to create more inclusive institutions, in which students, educators, and leaders all feel safe, welcome, and valued.

NEW DIRECTIONS FOR COMMUNITY COLLEGES, no. 179, Fall 2017 © 2017 Wiley Periodicals, Inc.
Published online in Wiley Online Library (wileyonlinelibrary.com) • DOI: 10.1002/cc.20266

Current Gender Issues

The 2016 election year was marked with hope that the glass ceiling would be shattered and the first woman president would be elected. Instead, a backlash occurred in which women's rights and those of marginalized populations such as immigrants, citizens of color, and LGBTQ populations are at risk. To counter the challenges facing these historically marginalized groups, the public rhetoric instead highlights "progress." For example, a recent report by Equilar ("Boards Will Reach," 2017), a corporate research firm, has been widely published in newspapers across the nation touting women's progress in business. Presently, women make up 15.1% of all directors seats at publicly traded U.S. companies, which represents an increase to be sure, but equity will not be reached until 2055 at the current pace. As in other arenas, community colleges show more headway in terms of inclusivity as women comprise nearly 34% of 2-year colleges boards of trustees (Moltz, 2009), which is the highest in postsecondary education. However, despite the fact that one in three board members are women, a full 82% of board members are White. Diversity is elusive on boards, as it is in leadership and faculty ranks in community colleges. Though progress can be lauded in the community college sector, even here equity is absent.

It is against this national backdrop that emerging gender issues facing community colleges occur. Because of the fast pace of change by the new president in the first days of 2017, the extent to which legislative actions may move against women and minorities remains unknown. Early actions, however, signal concern with the reinstatement by Executive Order of the Global Gag Rule that limits information sharing on reproductive options (Girard, 2017) and the rescinding of rules for transgender bathrooms (Peters, Becker, & Davis, 2017). Despite the future uncertainty of federal activity, several salient issues have emerged that require attention. First, the overall neoliberal and corporate approaches to education affect the foci of community colleges, including areas of access, performance, and strategic planning. Second, Title IX is under continued attack, which creates uncertainty in the ways in which this act will continue to shape gender policies on campus. Progress on policies regarding sexual assault on campus is tenuous given the change in U.S. cabinet positions to a cabinet that now consists of mostly White men (Lee, 2017). Pointedly, newly installed Secretary of Education Betsy DeVos signaled "the likelihood of a significant shift in federal policy on sexual assault in college" (Anderson, 2017, para. 1) during her confirmation hearings. Third, the use of intersectionality helps to expand constructions of gender and campus programs supporting students and professionals with multiple identities have shown progress. Finally, the persistence of the glass ceiling underscores the need for deep cultural change to occur for equity and inclusiveness to become ubiquitous. On a positive note, the tipping point for change is beginning to occur on some campuses and these examples can serve as a model for others.

Neoliberal Influence.   In a study of community college mission statements, Ayers (2005) found that a neoliberal discourse had taken hold in the sector. These orientations give preference to corporate values over academic norms and reward economic outcomes over those supporting the public good. As a result, tensions emerge when accountability demands counter the open access mission of community colleges and when decisions are made to increase completion rates at the expense of inclusivity (Bragg & Durham, 2012). Because community colleges enroll the largest percentage of minority students (Snyder & Dillow, 2013), a focus on the end goal of completion can threaten these enrollments. For example, research highlights greater academic risks for minorities relative to their White counterparts in college, including entering college less prepared academically, facing institutional barriers and cultures in which microaggressions are common, and juggling financial challenges and family responsibilities (Greene, Marti, & McClenney, 2008; Wood, 2012). What is often missing with a change in focus to completion are programs to help support minority men, thus the program benefits outlined by Dawn Person and colleagues in Chapter 6 are particularly important in today's community colleges. Critical theory provides an alternative means to counter the pervasive rhetoric of neoliberalism and points out the need to continue resisting a deficit model in thinking about minorities in education (Patton, 2016).

A focus on the bottom line and completion rates can lead to a time of crisis for community colleges. Paradoxically, when colleges are in crisis it is more likely that women are chosen to lead the institution versus men. Haslam and Ryan (2008) coined the term *glass cliff* to describe this phenomenon. In times of crisis, more women are selected as leaders as there is a greater risk of failure for the institution. When women accept positions to help community colleges in jeopardy, they have an opportunity to showcase their talents, but they are often hobbled by the context, just as some of the presidents highlighted in Chapter 3 discussed.

To combat the negative effects of the omnipresent nature of neoliberalism in community colleges, it is important to challenge the norms that dictate behavior. Ayers (2005) advocated the creation of a counterhegemonic discourse to take place in community colleges. In this case, individuals can work to create discourse that challenges the acceptance of neoliberalism but also instigates discourse to challenge narrow views of gender as merely men or women. Instead, the challenging discourse that needs to occur must focus on pointing out faulty assumptions of seeing gender as a binary and of anticipating certain roles for individuals based on their gender.

Social Construction of Gender.   The social construction of gender occurs through ongoing social interactions (Berger & Luckmann, 1966). In this case, gender can be constructed in a variety of ways, including individually based ideals of gender. But, the sex categories presented at birth are reinforced in different ways over the lifespan. Expanded constructions of gender help to move beyond binary views of gender. But a move in this fashion requires changes in the ways individuals interact to reinforce wider definitions of gender.

Transgender students' concerns are one issue in the forefront on college campuses as these individuals demand a place in community colleges. Not only are gender-neutral bathrooms an issue (Brown, 2005) but also safe spaces on campus. Student affairs practitioners play a large role in advocating for trans* students. Marine (2017) argued that "trickle up social justice work requires a willingness to take an active stance on behalf of trans* students: To seek out their perspectives, to collect and analyze data rigorously and regularly, and to investigate the origins of current practices, including the myths that may circulate underneath and around them" (p. 253). As Zamani-Gallaher pointed out in Chapter 8, several community colleges have made progress in creating LGBTQ-friendly practices and policies.

Critical to the social construction of gender is acknowledgement of intersectionality of identities. Crenshaw (1991) first coined the construct of intersectionality. Since then, other scholars have explored this concept in college settings. Robbins and McGowan (2016) pointed out three key tenets of intersectionality as they argued for new approaches to student development theories:

1. Rejection of an additive approach to social inequality, a postpositivist assumption. Instead, identity is produced based on "the convergence of ability, class, ethnicity, gender, race, sexual orientation, and other social identities." (p. 76).
2. A holistic approach versus an individual orientation; thus there may be "multiple systems of oppression (for example, racism, genderism, and sexism)." (p. 76).
3. Systems of oppression are not neutral, for instance, "intersectionality foregrounds activism, advocacy, and social movements." (p. 77)

Moving toward creating inclusive environments on community college campuses requires attention to the ways in which student affairs practitioners, campus leaders, educators, and students are addressing intersectionality. Complicating constructions of gender involves rejecting the traditional concept of viewing gender as a binary and provides new ways to think about gender.

Title IX.   In 1972, Title IX was passed into federal law prohibiting discrimination on the basis of sex in any federally funded education program or activity. The historical importance of the law focused on providing women access to higher education and opportunities to participate in athletics. For current millennial students, the importance of this type of access seems like ancient history, but for those of us who lived through the era of implementation of Title IX, the legislation was groundbreaking. Community colleges provided critical access to higher education for women in these early days of the law. This type of access remains important to vast majorities to this day.

More recently, attention to Title IX has focused on campus sexual assault policies. As Lee reviewed in Chapter 5, the Clery Act requires reporting of information on campus crime statistics. The Campus Sexual Violence Elimination (SaVE) Act amended the Clery Act in 2013 to provide transparency on campus about incidents of sexual violence, guarantees victims enhanced rights, sets standards for disciplinary proceedings, and requires campus-wide prevention education programs. Community colleges are not exempt from these requirements, but given their resources and size, meeting these requirements often stretches them. Exemplars help navigate compliance with the law.

Community colleges often provide resources to students and staff that they do not have in their private lives. Creating safe learning environment is indeed incumbent on each of us, especially when these policies are under attack and the future is unknown.

Persistent Glass Ceilings.   Hymowitz and Schellhardt (1986) first coined the term glass ceiling to refer to the invisible barrier for women trying to get to the top rungs of leadership. In part, this barrier is a result of women being judged by male-based ideal worker norms (Williams, 2000). The existence of ideal worker norms sets up a false sense of equity in the workplace. On the one hand, women are advised that if they only worked harder (i.e., like men do) and "lean in" (Sandberg, 2013), they will have a place at the table. On the other hand, entrenched masculinized ideal worker norms persist even when workplace accommodations are made to counter these expectations and provide more flexible work environments (Kelly, Ammons, Chermack, & Moen, 2015). The expectation that work takes precedence over family or other life responsibilities continues to assume that employees can focus solely on work because someone else is fulfilling work on the home front (Acker, 1990; Williams, 2000).

Here, ideal worker norms present a restricted depiction of acceptable behavior for women faculty and leaders (Williams, 2000). Pointedly, the women faculty in Ward and Wolf-Wendel's (Chapter 4) longitudinal study picked the community college setting for the flexibility they perceived in being able to work and have a family and more balanced life. Yet, these same women do not sense that community colleges remain "good places to work" when advancing in leadership ranks.

Breaking the glass ceiling can occur when a tipping point is reached, however, which requires building a critical mass. Once a critical mass is reached, typically marked by at least 30% or more representation, change occurs (Burkinsaw, 2015). Martin and O'Meara (2017) reviewed changes in Maryland, which boosts women as presidents in 56% of the state's community colleges—almost double the national average of 33% women presidents in the 2-year sector (American Council on Education [ACE], 2012). This tipping point occurred in Maryland because of targeted leadership development and mentoring opportunities for women leaders, training for trustees, and a robust labor market for presidential spouses. These outcomes are encouraging as they show how positive change can occur through concerted efforts. If the other 49 states instituted similar programs, the glass ceiling would finally break.

Strategies for Changing Practice

Change is the word of the day. This section provides strategies that various stakeholders can employ to help begin, support, and institutionalize change in practice. Change theory underscores the need to establish urgency for change and to obtain buy-in for larger scale changes (Kezar, 2014; Kotter, 2014). How change occurs may differ by stakeholder group, but it is critical to understand the intersectionality of groups, issues, and strategies. The final portion of this section underscores how policy changes can occur to support stakeholders and address organizational issues.

Students.   Gender construction is particularly salient for traditionally aged college students as they enter important identity development stages during their college years (Evans, Forney, Guiddo, Patton, & Renn, 2010). Moving conversations about identity development from singular views of gender and instead envisioning gender construction as a matrix (Baca Zinn, Hondagneu-Sotelo, & Messner, 2010) provides a more complex perspective of gender identity that allows for intersections. Some community college campuses have diversity offices or women's centers, but they are few in number. As a result, students require a forum or space in which to learn about gender identity and to discuss questions they may have both personally and about how to support friends. The increased availability of resources online provides a wider net of assistance for students, yet trusted allies on campus are also needed. Individually, students can learn more about gender and identity via these resources and in discussion with campus support offices.

In their advocacy for expanded conceptualization of student development theory, Robbins and McGowan (2016) provided a range of ways that students and campuses could become more inclusive. Students can create spaces in which they can discuss and explore identity, particularly identity conflicts. The use of inclusive language that remains gender neutral can provide recognition of the full spectrum of gender identities on campus. Not only can marginalized students advocate for support, they can enlist allies in their efforts. Often, a part of this advocacy is educating others on the issues. As Zamani-Gallaher reviewed in Chapter 8, it is important for those with cisprivilege to recognize the advantages they have and how LGBTQ students do not experience college in the same ways.

Different classroom experiences also emerge based on gender. A key area for students is selection of major or program. In spite of decades of effort, women are still underrepresented in traditional male-dominated professions like science, technology, engineering, and math (STEM) and vocational trades such as construction or welding. The National Science Foundation's (NSF) *Women, Minorities, and Persons with Disabilities in Science and Engineering Report* (2017) found that a gap persists in STEM educational attainment between underrepresented minorities and Whites and Asians. Even though White men make up only one third of the nation's population, they hold half of science and engineering jobs. Despite NSF funding for a range of programs to help increase the STEM pipeline, in particular for women and minorities, real progress has been elusive. Establishing interest in these majors, however, needs to occur prior to enrollment at the community college. In this case, links with teachers and students in elementary and secondary schools help increase the pipeline and interest in pursuing STEM majors and careers.

Issues of safety on campus are important for all students, but in particular for women and LGBTQ students. Students must know reporting requirements for sexual assault on campus and where to seek help. Peer counseling helps those who have been victims of sexual assault, which in community colleges may occur both on and off campus. Student affairs offices can aid in supporting and instilling individual agency for students to help prevent assaults and to know their rights. Blatant attacks on individuals represent only one safety concern, as microaggressions, racial profiling, and implicit bias are insidious and often harder for students to identify and to know how to deal with the outcomes.

Faculty.   Despite the equity evident in initial hires in faculty ranks, differences exist based on full-time versus part-time status. Increasingly, the diminishing numbers of full-time faculty on campus place a heavy load on full-time faculty. Institutions need to study the composition of campus committees to confirm equity in representation and to ensure that some groups are not being overworked whereas others have power advantage. On the one hand, community colleges are perceived as good places to work. On the other hand, little information exists regarding how gender nonconforming faculty perceive 2-year colleges. We know that White women enjoy the flexibility afforded by working in community colleges, but what can encourage others to pursue careers in the sector?

A persistent faculty issue is the lack of diversity in faculty ranks. A paradox is evident in that community colleges enroll large numbers of minorities, but these students have few faculty role models who look like them. Current faculty can plant a seed with students about career options as future faculty to help broaden representation in faculty ranks. Diversity here can occur both in terms of increasing the number of faculty of color and also in increasing the number of women in traditional male disciplines. Hosting panels of alumni who have pursued these types of careers and faculty telling their story of how they arrived in their roles can help. Illustrating the pathway to faculty roles can provide a critical step to broadening diversity in faculty ranks.

Midlevel leadership, including faculty leadership, should receive more attention on campus. The flattening of organizational hierarchies requires increased roles for all employees. The push for networked leadership (Eddy, Sydow, Alfred, & Garza Mitchell, 2015) assumes that faculty members provide a critical linchpin in organizational leadership and change. If women are opting out of seeking top-level positions, it is important to provide more support and development opportunities. Perhaps most important, it is necessary to reshape what it means to be a faculty leader and to question organizational architecture that gives preference to only one form of leading. Absent from many conversations of faculty roles is how to leverage the involvement of part-time faculty beyond thinking of them as low-cost alternatives to instruction that help the bottom line of the budget.

Leadership.   Current leaders can help change inclusivity in institutions. As evident in the example about the case in Maryland (Martin & O'Meara, 2017), change is possible when policies and supports are in place to broaden the leadership pipeline. Change requires leadership on multiple fronts, including boards of trustees who serve as gatekeepers to presidential hiring, current leaders who provide leadership development opportunities to potential future leaders, and midlevel leaders who support and promote inclusivity. Merely telling women or minorities to just try harder blames the individual. Instead, institutions need to investigate what unexamined barriers exist that prevent individuals from seeking advancement. Often, second-generation bias is in operation.

Second-generation bias differs from first-generation bias that involves overt discrimination. Instead, second-generation bias emerges in subtle forms that involve "patterns of interaction, informal norms, networking, mentoring, and evaluation" (Sturm, 2001, p. 458) that create norms and expectations of what leaders look like and how they act—which is based on White male norms. Combating these invisible biases is difficult. It is important to educate potential leaders about these forms of second generation bias so they can first be aware of their existence and second so they can combat and address these biases. Creating spaces for women and underrepresented individuals to test leading and developing leadership skills becomes important to achieving inclusivity in top positions. This type of preparation helps in the transition to larger roles within the college (Ibarra, Ely, & Kolb, 2013). Recognizing that women desire a sense of purpose in leading and collaborating begins to change the way leadership is conceived and normed.

Higher education has done a poor job in thinking about leadership succession planning. True, the American Association of Community Colleges (AACC) has developed a set of competencies deemed important to lead in the 2-year sector and has offered leadership institutes to prepare emerging leaders (AACC, 2013). But this is not enough. It is important in moving forward to rethink leadership and how we picture leaders. By opening up the pipeline and preparing a broad range of individuals for leading, more diverse thinking can emerge. Succession planning in college settings differs from the corporate world as individuals are not groomed to take over within the college. However, thinking about succession planning as a sector issue can change how we prepare tomorrow's leaders. Training and developing individuals to take on more responsibility in house can hone leadership skills and aptitude for seeing the bigger picture of college operations. About one third of college presidents are promoted from within (ACE, 2012), so investment in this type of development can pay off. Critically, the majority of presidents must move to take over new positions, but they must be prepared along the way. Thus, investing internally in talent development may not ensure a successor at the institution delivering the training, but it still benefits the sector as a whole.

Another forum for developing leaders is in graduate programs. It has long been recognized that the doctorate is viewed as a requirement for top-level positions (Townsend & Bassoppo-Moyo, 1997) and is increasingly becoming desirable in midlevel leader searches too. More than providing a credential, graduate programs can prepare curriculum and programs to better support future leaders (Eddy, 2009). It is important that we reach a tipping point in which it is not unusual to have women or underrepresented individuals leading community colleges.

Policy.   Institutions need to conduct a self-study of current policies to determine hidden barriers that prevent inclusivity on campus. Changes to policy can remove hurdles for faculty, administrators, and students. Overarching policies that are family friendly alleviate the need for individuals to negotiate on their own and help assure equity in the process. These policies need to be structured in a way that is gender neutral to accommodate the intersections of gender and identity in the workplace. Family-friendly policies can address childcare centers and diversity offices that provide support and safe spaces for campus members.

Other areas for policy improvement can focus on hiring practices, leave policies, and gender policies for reporting assault or acts of discriminations. Signaling support for expanded conceptions of gender by supporting minority men programs, developing processes to broaden the leadership pipeline, and taking quick action against acts of violence on campus begin to change the campus culture. Setting out models of good practice can begin to have influence beyond the campus as well.

Although fiscal pressures are a reality for campuses, not all programs of support need to be offered solely at the college. Instead, colleges can leverage programing with community partners and other educational institutions to provide needed services at a lower cost. Out of these arrangements can grow other types of connections for the college that help fulfill their broad mission. It is important to acknowledge the influence of the colleges within the state and to have community colleges advocate state and federal policies that allow full protection and support of underrepresented populations.

Conclusion

Taking a look back in time on changes regarding gender in community colleges shows some progress, but pointedly, nagging issues remain and new challenges have emerged. Community colleges provide a unique context for hope as long-standing institutions of second chances. It is important that they remain at the forefront as welcoming sites for a wide range of people representing an array of gender intersections and help in upholding the rights of women, LGBTQ populations, persons of color, and immigrants looking for ways to improve their lives. Moving forward, intersectionality provides new ways to consider the construction of gender, and therefore new ways to support campus members. Simply thinking that a few programs or policies will resolve campus problems is not enough; instead, more active engagement is required by all campus members to make community colleges more inclusive.

References

Acker, J. (1990). Hierarchies, jobs, bodies: A theory of gendered organization. *Gender & Society, 4*, 139–158.

American Association of Community Colleges. (2013). *AACC competencies for community college leaders* (2nd ed.). Washington, DC: Author. Retrieved from http://www.aacc.nche.edu/newsevents/Events/leadershipsuite/Documents/AACC_Core_Competencies_web.pdf

American Council on Education. (2012). *The American college president: 2012 edition.* Washington, DC: Author.

Anderson, N. (2017, January 18). Under DeVos, Education Department likely to make significant shift on sexual assault. *Washington Post.* Retrieved from https://www.washingtonpost.com/news/grade-point/wp/2017/01/18/under-devos-education-department-likely-to-make-significant-shift-on-sexual-assault/?utm_term=.ef858133a575

Ayers, D. F. (2005). Neoliberal ideology in community college mission statements: A critical discourse analysis. *Review of Higher Education, 28*(4), 527–549.

Baca Zinn, M., Hondagneu-Sotelo, P., & Messner, M. A. (2010). *Gender through the prism of difference* (4th ed.). New York, NY: Oxford University Press

Berger, P. L., & Luckmann, T. (1966). *The social construction of reality: A treatise in the sociology of knowledge.* Garden City, NY: First Anchor.

Blythe, A. (2016, March 28). NC transgender law draws lawsuit; Gov. Pat McCrory goes on the offense. *News & Observer.* Retrieved from http://www.newsobserver.com/news/politics-government/state-politics/article68603702.html

Boards will reach gender parity in 2055 at current pace. (2017, January). *Equilar Blog.* Retrieved from http://www.equilar.com/blogs/212-boards-will-reach-gender-parity-in-2055.html

Bragg, D. D., & Durham, B. (2012). Perspectives on access and equity in the era of (community) college completion. *Community College Review, 40*(2), 106–125.

Brown, P. L. (2005, March). The quest for a bathroom that's neither a men's nor a women's room. *New York Times.* Retrieved from http://www.nytimes.com/2005/03/04/us/a-quest-for-a-bathroom-thats-neither-mens-room-nor-womens-room.html

Burkinsaw, P. (2015). *Higher education, leadership and women vice chancellors: Fitting into communities of practice of masculinities*. London, UK: Palgrave Macmillan.

Cho, S., Crenshaw, K. W., & McCall, L. (2013). Toward a field of intersectionality studies: Theory, applications, and praxis. *Signs: Journal of Women in Culture and Society*, 38(4), 785–810.

Crenshaw, K. (1991). Mapping the margins: Intersectionality, identity politics, and violence against women of color. *Stanford Law Review*, 43(6), 1241–1299.

Eddy, P. L. (2009). Changing of the guard in community colleges: The role of leadership development. In A. Kezar (Ed.), *Rethinking leadership in a complex, multicultural, and global environment: New concepts and models for higher education* (pp. 185–211). Sterling, VA: Stylus Press.

Eddy, P. L., & Lester, J. (2008). Strategizing for the future. In J. Lester (Ed.), *New Directions in Community Colleges: No. 142. Gendered perspectives on community colleges* (pp. 107–116). San Francisco, CA: Jossey-Bass.

Eddy, P. L., Sydow, D. L., Alfred, R. L., & Garza Mitchell, R. L. (2015). *Developing tomorrow's leaders: Contexts, challenges, and capabilities*. Lanham, MD: Rowman & Littlefield.

Evans, N. J., Forney, D. S., Guido, F. M., Patton, L. D., & Renn, K. S. (2010). *Student development in college: Theory, research, and practice* (2nd ed.). San Francisco, CA: Jossey-Bass.

Girard, F. (2017). Implications of the Trump administration for sexual and reproductive rights globally. *Reproductive Health Matters*, 25(49), 1–8. https://doi.org/10.1080/09688080.2017.1301028

Greene, T. G., Marti, C. N., & McClenney, K. (2008). The effort–outcome gap: Differences for African American and Hispanic community college students in student engagement and academic achievement. *Journal of Higher Education*, 79(5), 513–539.

Haslam, S. A., & Ryan, M. K. (2008). The road to the glass cliff: Differences in the perceived suitability of men and women for leadership positions in succeeding and failing organizations. *Leadership Quarterly*, 19(5), 530–546.

Hymowitz, C., & Schellhardt, T. D. (1986, March 24). The glass ceiling: Why women can't seem to break the invisible barrier that blocks them from the top jobs. *Wall Street Journal*, 61.

Ibarra, H., Ely, R., & Kolb, D. (2013). Women rising: The unseen barriers. *Harvard Business Review*, 91(9), 60–66.

Kelly, E. L., Ammons, S. K., Chermack, K., & Moen, P. (2015). Gendered challenge, gendered response: Confronting the ideal worker norm in a white-collar organization. *Gender & Society*, 24(3), 281–303.

Kezar, A. J. (2014). *How colleges change: Understanding, leading, and enacting change*. New York, NY: Routledge.

Kotter, J. P. (2014). *Accelerate: Building strategic agility for a faster-moving world*. Boston, MA: Harvard Business Review Press.

Lee, J. C. (2017, March 17). Trump's cabinet so far is more white and male than any first cabinet since Reagan's. *New York Times*. Retrieved from https://www.nytimes.com/interactive/2017/01/13/us/politics/trump-cabinet-women-minorities.html

Marine, S. B. (2017). Trans* college students: Moving beyond inclusion. In P. L. Eddy, K. Ward, & T. Khwaja (Eds.), *Critical approaches to women and gender in higher education* (pp. 237–257). New York, NY: Palgrave.

Martin, A., & O'Meara, K. A. (2017). Conditions enabling women's leadership in community colleges. In P. L. Eddy, K. Ward, & T. Thwaja (Eds.), *Critical approaches to women and gender in higher education* (pp. 61–86). New York, NY: Palgrave.

Moltz, D. (2009, April). Who are community college trustees? *Inside Higher Ed*. Retrieved from https://www.insidehighered.com/news/2009/04/06/acct

National Science Foundation. (2017). *Women, minorities, and persons with disabilities in science and engineering report.* Washington, DC: Author. Retrieved from https://nsf.gov/statistics/2017/nsf17310/

Patton, L. D. (2016). Disrupting postsecondary prose: Toward a critical race theory of higher education. *Urban Education, 51*(3), 315–342.

Peters, J. W., Becker, J., & Davis, J. H. (2017, February 22). Trump rescinds rules on bathrooms for transgender students. *New York Times,* A1. Retrieved from https://www.nytimes.com/2017/02/22/us/politics/devos-sessions-transgender-students-rights.html

Robbins, C. K., & McGowan, B. L. (2016). Intersectional perspectives on gender and gender identity development. In E. S. Abes (Ed.), *New Directions for Student Services: No. 154. Critical perspectives on student development theory* (pp. 71–83). San Francisco, CA: Jossey-Bass.

Sandberg, S. (2013). *Lean in: Women, work, and the will to lead.* New York, NY: Alfred A. Knopf/Random House.

Snyder, T. D., & Dillow, S. A. (2013). *Digest of education statistics 2013.* Washington, DC: National Council on Education Statistics.

Sturm, S. (2001). Second generation employment discrimination: A structural approach. *Columbia Law Review, 101*(3), 458–568.

Townsend, B. K. (Ed.). (1995). *New Directions for Community Colleges: No. 89. Gender and power in the community college.* San Francisco, CA: Jossey-Bass.

Townsend, B. K., & Bassoppo-Moyo, S. (1997). The effective community college academic administrator: Necessary competencies and attitudes. *Community College Review, 25*(2), 41–56.

Williams, J. C. (2000). *Unbending gender.* New York, NY: Oxford University.

Wood, J. L. (2012). Bottom line: From the right to fail to the right to succeed: Black males in community colleges. *About Campus, 17,* 30–32. https://doi.org/10.1002/abc.21078

PAMELA L. EDDY *is a professor of higher education and department chair of Educational Policy, Planning, and Leadership at the College of William & Mary. Her research focuses on community college leadership, gender, and faculty development.*

NEW DIRECTIONS FOR COMMUNITY COLLEGES • DOI: 10.1002/cc

INDEX

Clery, Jeanne, 60
Climate of inclusivity, creation of, 18
Coates, C. A., 61, 64, 65
Cohen, A. M., 90
Collaborative decision making, 26
Collado, H., 14
College Equality Index (CEI), 93
Communication, role of, for women
 leaders: approach used in study, 256;
 findings from study, 25–30; future
 research, recommendations for, 32–
 33; gendered communication and, 26–
 28; institutional leaders, recommendations for, 31–32; pay inequity and,
 29; physical appearance and, 28–29;
 study on, 24–33; woman's relationships and, 30; women leaders, recommendations for, 30–31
Communicative team, 31
Community college: as feminized work
 spaces, 55
Community colleges, 12; chilly classroom climates at, 13; gender and leadership at, 16–17; gender inequity in,
 12–15; gender performance and masculinity, 15–16; leaders, 31–32; men of
 color in, 13–15; suggestions for ways
 to change practices, 17–18; women in,
 status of, 12–13
Cook, B., 77
Corporate values, 103
Cote, D., 68
Cox, E. M., 13, 16, 94
Crenshaw, K. W., 101, 104

Daniels, J. R., 16, 18
Davis, J. H., 102
Dawson, R., 67, 75
deBeauvoir, S., 39
de Brey, C., 89
Demers, A. L., 77, 80
Denissen, A. M., 67
De Sawal, D. M., 77–79, 81
de Tocqueville, A., 35
Dillow, S. A., 41, 101, 103
DiRamio, D., 77–81
Dobbins, N., 68
"Doing gender," concept of, 23–24
Donovan, J., 50
Downing-Matibag, T. M., 73
Drake, E., 48, 49
Dunlop Velez, E., 89
Durham, B., 103
Dutra, L., 78–80

Eddy, P. L., 13, 16, 17, 31, 37, 43, 48, 49,
 56, 94, 101, 108, 109, 112
Edison, M. I., 13
Edwards, A. F., 23, 34
Ely, R., 108
Employment, social status, and mas-
 culinity, relationship between, 15
Engleberg, I., 31
Equilar (research firm), 102
Equity Scorecard Project, 17
Evans, N. J., 106

Faculty, in community colleges, 47; re-
 search on, 49. See also Women faculty,
 in community college
Family responsibilities, 30, 32, 54
Feldman, J., 78, 79
Female-oriented leadership: perceptions
 of, 16; traits, 16
Feminism, 24–25; and choice, 49–50;
 liberal, 50, 55; poststructural view of,
 50, 55
Ferguson, A., 50
Forney, D. S., 106
Foss, K. A., 24
Foss, S. K., 24
Foster, L. K., 80
Fox, K. A., 59, 62, 63
Fry, R., 14

Galupo, M. P., 97
García, Y., 67, 76
Gardella, J. H., 61, 64, 65
Gardenshire-Crooks, A., 14
Garza Mitchell, R. L., 43, 48, 49, 56,
 108
Gasman, M., 18
Gender: cisgender privilege, 92–94; in
 community colleges settings, 94–96;
 current gender issues, 102–106; and
 faculty diversity, 90–91; identity and
 expression, 91; naming of, 91–92; so-
 cial construction of, 103–104; and stu-
 dent diversity, 89–90
Gendered   communication,   26–28,
 30
Gender harassment, 79
Gender identity, construction of, 23
Gender inequities, 11–12. See also Com-
 munity colleges
Gender performance: and masculinity,
 15–16; research on, 15
Genderqueer, 92
Gendron, J., 78, 79